Arson

by Gail B. Stewart

LUCENT BOOKS

An imprint of Thomson Gale, a part of The Thomson Corporation

THOMSON

GALE

Detroit • New York • San F... • London • Munich

ˎ Acknowledgement

We would like to express our sincere gratitude to criminalist, Jennifer Shen, of the San Diego Police Department crime lab for her invaluable review of Lucent's Crime Scene Investigations: *Arson.*

© 2006 Thomson Gale, a part of The Thomson Corporation.

Thomson and Star Logo are trademarks and Gale and Lucent Books are registered trademarks used herein under license.

For more information, contact
Lucent Books
27500 Drake Rd.
Farmington Hills, MI 48331-3535
Or you can visit our Internet site at http://www.gale.com

LIBRARY OF CONGRESS CATALOGING-IN-PUBLICATION DATA

Stewart, Gail, 1949–
 Arson / by Gail B. Stewart.
  p. cm. — (Crime Scene Investigations)
 Includes bibliographical references and index.
 ISBN 1-59018-617-6 (hard cover : alk. paper)
 1. Arson investigation—Juvenile literature. 2. Arson—Juvenile literature. I. Title. II. Series.
HV8079.A7S83 2005
363.25'964—dc22
 	
                                                                     2004030550

Printed in the United States of America

Contents

Foreword

The popularity of crime scene and investigative crime shows on television has come as a surprise to many who work in the field. The main surprise is the concept that crime scene analysts are the true crime solvers, when in truth, it takes dozens of people, doing many different jobs, to solve a crime. Often, the crime scene analyst's contribution is a small one. One Minnesota forensic scientist says that the public "has gotten the wrong idea. Because I work in a lab similar to the ones on *CSI*, people seem to think I'm solving crimes left and right—just me and my microscope. They don't believe me when I tell them that it's the investigators that are solving crimes, not me."

Crime scene analysts do have an important role to play, however. Science has rapidly added a whole new dimension to gathering and assessing evidence. Modern crime labs can match a hair of a murder suspect to one found on a murder victim, for example, or recover a latent fingerprint from a threatening letter, or use a powerful microscope to match tool marks made during the wiring of an explosive device to a tool in a suspect's possession.

Probably the most exciting of the forensic scientist's tools is DNA analysis. DNA can be found in just one drop of blood, a dribble of saliva on a toothbrush, or even the residue from a fingerprint. Some DNA analysis techniques enable scientists to tell with certainty, for example, whether a drop of blood on a suspect's shirt is that of a murder victim.

While these exciting techniques are now an essential part of many investigations, they cannot solve crimes alone. "DNA doesn't come with a name and address on it," says the Minnesota forensic scientist. "It's great if you have someone in custody to match the sample to, but otherwise, it doesn't help. That's the investigator's job. We can have all the great DNA evidence in the world, and without a suspect, it will just sit on the shelf. We've all seen cases with very little forensic evidence get solved by the resourcefulness of a detective."

While forensic specialists get the most media attention today, the work of detectives still forms the core of most criminal investigations. Their job, in many ways, has changed little over the years. Most cases are still solved through the persistence and determination of a criminal detective whose work may be anything but glamorous. Many cases require routine, even mind-numbing tasks. After the July 2005 bombings in London, for example, police officers sat in front of video players watching thousands of hours of closed-circuit television tape from security cameras throughout the city, and as a result were able to get the first images of the bombers.

The Lucent Books Crime Scene Investigations series explores the variety of ways crimes are solved. Titles cover particular crimes such as murder, specific cases such as the killing of three civil rights workers in Mississippi, or the role specialists such as medical examiners play in solving crimes. Each title in the series demonstrates the ways a crime may be solved, from the various applications of forensic science and technology to the reasoning of investigators. Sidebars examine both the limits and possibilities of the new technologies and present crime statistics, career information, and step-by-step explanations of scientific and legal processes.

The Crime Scene Investigations series strives to be both informative and realistic about how members of law enforcement—criminal investigators, forensic scientists, and others—solve crimes, for it is essential that student researchers understand that crime solving is rarely quick or easy. Many factors—from a detective's dogged pursuit of one tenuous lead to a suspect's careless mistakes to sheer luck to complex calculations computed in the lab are all part of crime solving today.

"I Can't Think of Anything More Terrible"

Cora still has trouble talking about the fire, even though it happened almost five years ago. She wraps her arms around her two daughters as she remembers the night they narrowly escaped with their lives.

"We were living in an apartment on the South side [of Chicago]," she says. "It was me and my two babies—they were one and two then. I woke up because I heard one of the babies coughing, crying 'Mama,' you know. I sat up and man! It hit me—I was smelling smoke. That was always the one thing I was afraid of in that building—it was old, and the smoke detectors in the hallways were always down. Kids would steal the batteries out of them, and the landlords wouldn't do anything about it.

"Anyway, I ran into [the girls'] room and grabbed them out of the bed. Cici—she's the oldest—she was coughing and trying to put her head under the blankets. I grabbed them both and ran out in the hall—we were on the third floor, and I was yelling, 'Fire, fire!'"

"I Can't Express It in Words"

"I was screaming, and the girls were screaming, crying because their eyes were stinging from the smoke. Someone already called the fire department, and we could hear the sirens. We were standing outside—you could see the flames shooting out of windows and glass was breaking. I remember thinking nobody had shoes on, that I could see, and all that broken glass. God, it was so scary, I can't express it in words. Everybody just standing out there on the street at three in the morning, crying. People saying, 'And did so-and-so get out, did everyone make it?'"

Firefighters cut into the roof of a building in an attempt to combat a roaring blaze.

Though everyone got out of the building safely, Cora says, several of the apartments were destroyed. "There was no time to be taking anything but the clothes on our backs," she says. "Nobody had any idea to grab their purse or anything, you know? And we couldn't go back in there. Even the ones whose apartments weren't ruined had to leave that night. Some of us went to a shelter, others I think just went to stay with family or friends. We lost pretty much everything, but I was so grateful we were alive."

It was only a few days later that she heard that the fire had been intentionally set—and the anger and frustration set in. "I can't tell you how I felt," she says. "Furious, that's the best word. The rumor I heard was that some man set the fire to get back at someone who owed him money. But I don't know for sure. I do know that they didn't arrest anyone for doing that terrible thing. Nobody had to pay for ruining our home, destroying all the photograph albums I had, or the baby clothes for my girls, all our possessions. Yes, it makes me angry. Someone set that fire intentionally, and I can't think of anything more terrible than that."[1]

A Misunderstood Crime

According to Federal Bureau of Investigation statistics, about one-third of the fires that occur each year in the United States are intentionally set—as was the one that destroyed Cora's home. Arsonists set not only homes and apartments on fire, but also churches, businesses, automobiles, and even wilderness areas. In 2002, more than $1.4 billion worth of property damage resulted from arson.

But arson does not only destroy property. It is a crime that can result in injuries and death as well. The inhabitants of homes and apartments and firefighters can be victims. "It infuriates firefighters when we hear people talk about arson as a property crime," says Dan, a former volunteer firefighter. "Anyone who's ever been on a [fire] scene where there's been a fatality knows better. I've known guys who've been injured

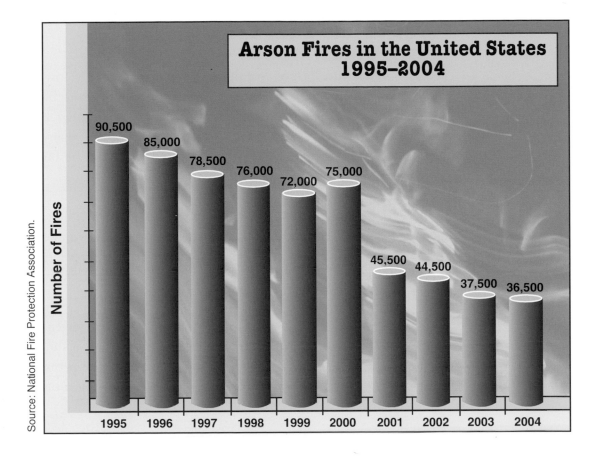

Arson Fires in the United States 1995–2004

Source: National Fire Protection Association.

Number of Fires

90,500 — 1995
85,000 — 1996
78,500 — 1997
76,000 — 1998
72,000 — 1999
75,000 — 2000
45,500 — 2001
44,500 — 2002
37,500 — 2003
36,500 — 2004

fighting fires that turned out to be set. It's like, you're risking your life, making sure the fire doesn't spread, or being sure everyone is out safe. It's a violent crime, and people who commit arson are felons. Period."[2]

Steve Avato, a special agent with the U.S. Bureau of Alcohol, Tobacco and Firearms (ATF), which investigates many arson cases, agrees wholeheartedly. He says that while people compare arson to homicide, setting fires can actually be far worse: "[I]f I shoot a gun at a person I intend to kill I might hit them or I may hit innocent victims. But there's limited damage a bullet can do; it will stop just by the laws of physics at some point. Fire will continue to burn as long as it has fuel and oxygen. . . . So unlike a bullet that will eventually stop, fire will just continue to burn and destroy whatever is in its path."[3]

The Crime That Destroys Its Own Clues

The success rate of convicting arsonists is extremely low. Because it is easy to start a fire and because arson tends to be a solitary crime, the chances are not very good that someone will be able to identify the arsonist. Even more troubling, many arsonists use timing devices to start fires, so they can be far away from the scene by the time anyone notices the flames.

Perhaps the most frustrating aspect of arson, however, is that it is the only violent crime that destroys its own evidence—at least a great deal of it. Not only do the flames and smoke consume much trace evidence that an arsonist might have left behind, but the water from firefighters' hoses can wash away

Although arson was originally suspected in the fire that raged through Crest, California, in 2003, the blaze was actually set by a lost hunter who was hoping to be rescued.

important clues, too. The scene must be meticulously worked to find clues, yet because of a burned building's exposure to the elements, arson investigators must do their work quickly, before evidence is destroyed.

It is little wonder that working a fire scene can seem to be an almost insurmountable task—at least to a beginner. One investigator recalls his first fire scene thirty years ago—a wool mill that had been burned to the ground: "It was dull, cold and raining. I stood on the ground floor of the ruined building, surrounded by carbonized debris and looked up at the sky and blackened beams from which water dripped to form steaming puddles at my feet. I recollect the question I asked myself, 'How can anyone extract useful information from this situation?'"[4]

DNA is extracted from cells and tested to determine whether it matches DNA found at the crime scene.

Arson investigators prepare to search for clues into the cause of a destructive church fire in Dumfries, Virginia.

Fortunately for law enforcement, arson investigation has improved a great deal in the past thirty years, thanks to advances in forensic science—the branch of science that establishes facts in criminal cases. Whether using technology to identify the chemical makeup of an accelerant or coaxing fingerprints and DNA out of the most unlikely places, forensic scientists make a crucial contribution to solving arson cases. Investigators have also made important advances in criminal profiling, learning more about what motivates arsonists. Yet even with the newest forensic tools and the most insightful psychological profiles, arson detectives face tremendous challenges in solving these dangerous and often deadly crimes.

CHAPTER 1

Establishing a Crime

Arson is a crime that is rarely solved on the spot. "Maybe somewhere there are cases where a passing patrol nabs a guy running from a fire with a gasoline can in his hand," says former fire chief Tom Hall, "or even better, where the guy runs into the guys with the nozzles fighting the fires! But I never had the pleasure of seeing an easy case like that. Arson cases are almost always time-consuming and require a lot of patience as you move step by step through the process."[5]

An Exterior Examination

The process of an arson investigation actually begins before it is certain whether a crime has been committed. Once a fire has been put out, every fire scene is carefully examined by a fire investigator, whose specific responsibility is to say how the fire started and whether a criminal investigation is called for.

Even before the fire scene is completely cool, an investigator can learn a great deal by what is called the exterior examination—gathering as much information as possible from the outside of the building. First of all, it is usually helpful to talk to the first firefighters who responded to the alarm. Even better, the person who called in the alarm can offer important information. Was there anyone leaving the scene quickly at the time of the fire? Did the witness see any cars around the building before the fire? If so, the investigator tries to get a detailed description of the person or vehicle.

"I've Got Some Video"

Information about the fire itself is valuable, too. An investigator asks where the flames and smoke were in the building. Did the witness notice what floor was on fire, or if the flames were reaching out the windows? Knowing where the fire originated is key to finding the cause, but by the time firefighters arrive, the fire has almost always spread, making it difficult for investigators to pinpoint the point of origin.

"It's really helpful if you can find someone who noticed the fire early," says one firefighter. "They can narrow things down, and that is unbelievably helpful. I was at a scene a few months ago where the entire building was on fire, and all of a sudden, someone comes up and says, 'Hey, I called it in, and I've got some video I took while the place was burning.' The guy admitted he was worried telling us, because he didn't want anyone to think he was ghoulish—like maybe he thought we'd think he really was excited about the fire. But, hey, we were grateful. I've talked to other [firefighters] who have had the same experience. [Video] is a great tool."[6]

Water used to put out a fire can create problems for investigators by destroying evidence.

In February 1991, investigators in Philadelphia were aided by video when a thirty-eight-story office building burned, resulting in the deaths of three firefighters and a cost of $400 million. The video allowed investigators to narrow their search for the origin of the blaze to one corner of a particular floor. "We knew early on," says investigator John Malooly, "that the fire began on the twenty-second floor and spread upwards. We were fortunate in having a video taken by a passerby of the early stage of the fire. We did a freeze-frame on the video and counted the windows from the side of the building until we reached the one that had flames venting out of it."[7]

Smoke and Flames

Besides asking witnesses about the location of the fire in its early stages, an investigator is curious about the color of the smoke and flames. Knowing what the fire looked like after it began to spread is not helpful, says one firefighter, for then the color of smoke is merely a residue of what the fire is burning as it moves through the building and even later, when firefighters begin to spray it with water. "What you want to know is how the fire looked when it was first spotted," he explains. "What color were the flames—were they red, or more yellow? Red or orange flames are less hot, which points away from arson. Arsonists usually use some product like gasoline, kerosene—something like that—to get the fire hot and fast, so that the structure gets destroyed quickly.

"On the other hand, lighter colors mean the flame was burning very hot—white being the hottest flame, usually over twenty-five hundred degrees or so. Any fire burning that hot at the beginning had help [in the form of accelerant]. And

Video footage can help investigators track where fires start and how they spread.

15

what was the smoke like? For example, if a witness to the fire in its early stages saw very white smoke with light yellow or white flame, that usually means that gasoline was used [as an accelerant]. On the other hand, if a witness saw flames that were deeper yellow, and the smoke was a brown color, it would point to a cooking fire—that's the color you associate with cooking oil. If you're lucky enough to have a witness that noticed details like that, it can help us learn about the fire before it spread through the building."[8]

Too-Helpful Witnesses

The exterior examination can also include looking at the witnesses themselves. Many arsonists enjoy watching the fires they set. It is not unusual for the arsonist to join a crowd of people watching the blaze as the firefighters try to control it. For that reason, some investigators insist that a photographer take video or still pictures of any people present at the fire scene.

Crowds watch as a historic building burns in Grahamstown, South Africa.

From Hero to Suspect

Arson investigators pay close attention to people who report or claim to have discovered a fire, or who want to be a part of the investigation or rescue effort—such people may be arsonists. In her 2003 Newsweek *article "The Hot Light of Heroism," Ellise Pierce describes one such case:*

A homeless high school dropout named Kris Leija told investigators that he had been biking through the streets of Abilene, Texas, early one morning, and had seen a fire in an apartment building. He fought smoke and flames to rescue four young children, and was immediately hailed as a hero. "I felt like God put me there for a reason," Leija told national television reporters.

But Leija's love of media attention made some arson experts suspicious. "You need to look at anyone who's repeatedly at the scene of fires," said one police officer, "and seems eager to get into the spotlight." Investigators did some research and found he had been involved in rescue efforts at another fire, just months before. Within a week of his appearance on *Good Morning America* and other news programs, Leija had become the number-one suspect in the fire.

Occasionally, a civilian may be quick to offer help to firefighters, either by providing information about the cause of the fire or by pinpointing the origin of the blaze. "Sadly, you have to take a closer look at those guys," says arson investigator Sean McKenna. "There is a whole category of fires known as 'vanity fires,' which are started by night watchmen, security guards, people like that. They want to be heroes, get respect by helping the police or the fire investigators. Sometimes they even run into the burning building to try and rescue someone."[9]

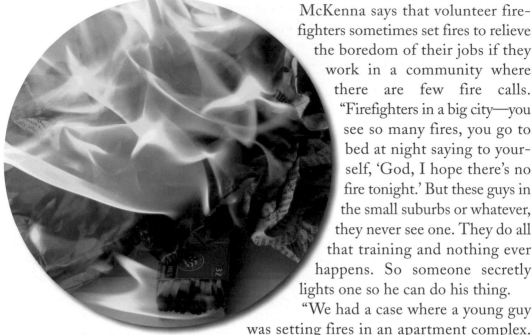

Investigators seek out signs of arson such as piles of newspapers or magazines used as fuel.

McKenna says that volunteer firefighters sometimes set fires to relieve the boredom of their jobs if they work in a community where there are few fire calls. "Firefighters in a big city—you see so many fires, you go to bed at night saying to yourself, 'God, I hope there's no fire tonight.' But these guys in the small suburbs or whatever, they never see one. They do all that training and nothing ever happens. So someone secretly lights one so he can do his thing.

"We had a case where a young guy was setting fires in an apartment complex. Lots of smoke, you couldn't see a thing. But this young guy, he and his crew always seemed to know just where to go in the building to find the fire really quick. Veteran crews were out there, stumbling around in the smoke—they don't know where to go, and they're saying, 'How is it this guy always can find the fire?' And it turned out that he was the one setting them. So as an investigator, you have to be aware of the people around you. You get to where certain kinds of behaviors, certain things raise little flags in your mind."[10]

Point of Origin

Once witness statements have been taken and the exterior of the structure examined, investigators proceed inside. The inside of a fire scene, says arson expert McKenna, often looks far worse than it really is. "Take a house fire—truly it looks very tragic to the owners, but most of the damage is from smoke and heat. The owners are seeing the damage to the furnishings—the chairs and couches, the wallpaper, things like that. But that stuff is of little use to the fire investigator.

"What we need to do, to find out what caused the fire, is to get right in the area of the most damage. That'll be where the fire started. We work on the theory that a fire burns hottest and longest at the point of origin. When you can find the 'where,' you can usually find the 'how'—or at least you can narrow it down to a couple of possibilities."[11]

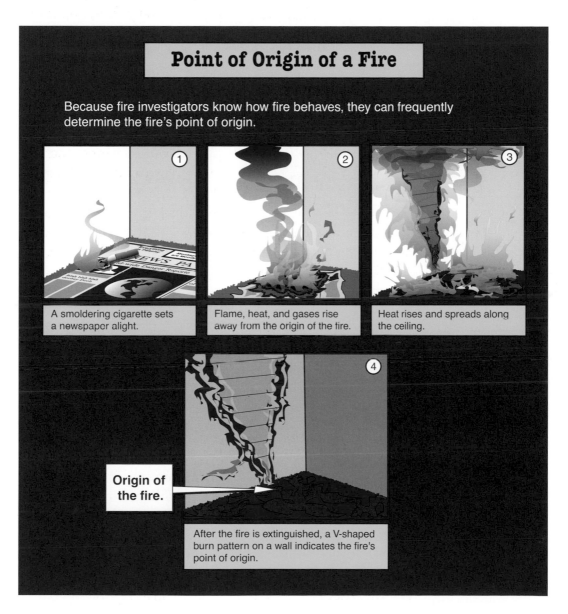

Point of Origin of a Fire

Because fire investigators know how fire behaves, they can frequently determine the fire's point of origin.

① A smoldering cigarette sets a newspaper alight.

② Flame, heat, and gases rise away from the origin of the fire.

③ Heat rises and spreads along the ceiling.

④ **Origin of the fire.**

After the fire is extinguished, a V-shaped burn pattern on a wall indicates the fire's point of origin.

Finding the point of origin is often a difficult job, but there are indicators in even the most ruined scenes that can help. Most important is a basic understanding of how fire behaves. The heat and gases move up, away from the origin of the blaze. The heat rises as high as it can in a room—usually until it hits the ceiling—and then gradually spreads out, igniting other combustibles as it travels.

Often this results in a V-shaped pattern of burn, which is evident on a wall. If a V-pattern can be seen, the bottom of the V virtually points to the area where the fire began. However, sometimes the pattern is not visible, or there has been too much damage to locate a V. In that case, there are other ways an investigator can discover the point of origin.

Alligator Skin and Bowing to the Fire God

Looking at wooden beams or heavy wooden furniture can often identify the path of the fire. It may be as simple a process as noting that one side is damaged more than the other side, which tells the investigator the direction the fire traveled from its source.

The damage to wood in a fire is a helpful indicator. As wood burns, its appearance changes. A burned oak beam or maple floor, for example, looks as though it is covered in scaly alligator skin. This material is called char, and an investigator can measure the amount of char (usually by sticking an ice pick in it) to discover how long that wood had been exposed to high heat. As investigators get closer to the fire's point of origin, the char becomes deeper, and the blisters or scales of the alligator skin become smaller and closer together.

Glass in the structure can also point to the fire's origin in a number of ways. Some window glass tends to become discolored by soot from the smoke during a fire. Scientists know, however, that the hotter the glass, the more active the molecules on the surface of the glass. Such molecular activity inhibits the amount of soot; consequently, the windows closest to the point of origin are free of soot.

Incandescent lightbulbs often break because of the extreme heat of a fire, but if an investigator is lucky enough to find one intact, it virtually points to the origin of the blaze. The glass exterior of the bulb becomes soft at 900°F (482°C), and as it melts, it curves toward the heat source. "You see the same thing in glass salt shakers and sometimes even a plastic milk jug," explains arson investigator McKenna. "They lean over towards the heat source—it's a strange phenomenon. We call it 'bowing to the fire god.'"[12]

Ruling Out Accidents

After locating the point of origin, fire investigators look for the cause of the fire—no easy task, since there are hundreds of reasons a fire might break out. Statistically, seven out of ten fires are caused by humans, although most of them are not arson. Instead, they can be attributed to carelessness or accidents. For a fire to be investigated as a possible arson, investigators must eliminate all accidental causes. Sometimes the cause is an easy one for an expert to spot—a clothes dryer that has overheated, for example, or a defective switch in the home's electrical system, or a gas pipe that leaked near a heating unit.

False Trails

Knowing where a fire started is the first step in pinpointing a fire's cause. But finding the fire's point of origin can be tricky even for the most experienced investigator. Conditions at the scene sometimes lead investigators on a false trail. The point of origin of a fire often shows the greatest amount of fire damage, but that is not always the case. In fact, several variables make it challenging for even the most experienced investigator to find the point of origin. For example, drafts from an open stairwell or window can influence the path of the fire. Also, the presence of stored chemicals such as gasoline, lighter fluid, or certain cleaning solvents can create a pocket of damage that may be confused with the point of origin. And an arsonist may deliberately set fires in various parts of a structure so that there are actually several points of origin.

Other fires are the result of a smoldering cigarette that falls onto a chair and ignites a cushion, or a candle that is placed too close to a curtain. Many others are caused by misuse of electrical cords or appliances. Each of these possible causes is checked off by the fire investigator viewing the point of the fire's origin.

"I ask myself questions when looking at a fire scene—and try right away to dispose of the most common scenarios," says McKenna.

Did someone overload an extension cord or try to plug in a three-prong socket into a two-prong outlet? Cords can get hot, and if they're twisted or they've been nicked by a vacuum cleaner, the exposed wire can smolder along a rug or chair or something. Was someone cooking here? That's a big source of fires—unattended cooking.

Evidence regarding the source of a fire may be found even in charred rubble.

I look for signs of a candle—either wax, a candle holder, even the little metal staple that holds the wick. Was someone doing welding, or was someone using some kind of machinery that can lead to fire—paint strippers, heat guns? Were there any motors or appliances going that malfunctioned or overheated—a slow cooker, a fan, something like that? Were there little kids in the house who could have had access to a lighter or matches? And in cases where there's a wildfire, I ask myself, could a passing train have kicked up a spark to start the grass on fire? And a biggie—a question that could be asked at any fire scene—was someone smoking here?[13]

By the Numbers

$4,000

Cost of property lost every minute as a result of an arson fire

Puddles, Stains, and Trailers

Occasionally, investigators find something in their initial walk-through that seems to be a likely sign of arson. Many arsonists believe that all traces of their crime will be destroyed in the fire, but that is not always the case. Investigators may discover the remains of a pile of newspapers, wood shavings, or rags that were used as fuel for the fire.

One of the most common tools used by an arsonist is an accelerant—a chemical such as gasoline or charcoal starter fluid that can speed up, or accelerate, the fire. An investigator may notice a suspicious stain on a floor or carpet at the point of origin. Further testing will determine whether the mark is evidence of arson, but investigators make note of the area.

Sometimes, too, an investigator finds material that has been placed near the accelerant to spread the fire from its point of origin. This is known as a "trailer" and may consist of gasoline-soaked towels or ropes tied end to end, long twists of newspaper, gunpowder, or trails of the accelerant itself. While these trailers do not usually survive intact, traces of them can sometimes be seen leading from the point of origin. If an investigator notices a long line of ash or material that is not completely burned, leading from what might be a stain of accelerant, it may be evidence of arson.

Possible Clues

Investigators also look for some sort of igniting device. Matches are probably the most common means of lighting a blaze, but there are others. Lit cigarettes and lighters are used, too. Although this type of evidence is often destroyed, occasionally a cigarette butt or packet of matches survives the blaze. If investigators see such remains at the point of origin, that, too, may point to arson as a cause of the fire.

A fire investigation officer searches for clues in the remains of a school fire.

Even when investigators find possible evidence that the fire was intentionally set, they still need to eliminate all possible accidental causes of the fire before they can declare it arson. "You can find a gasoline can in the room where the fire started," says former Minneapolis fire chief Tom Hall, "or you can find the remains of a candle, or any other evidence that points to arson. But that isn't enough. There are other reasons that stuff could be there, and there are cases where investigators have been wrong when they've jumped to conclusions."[14]

One such instance was a fire that was found to have started in the living room of a house. Investigators found traces of gasoline on the carpet—seemingly completely out of place. Though the presence of an accelerant seemed to strongly sug-

gest arson, information gathered during investigation proved otherwise. The house, it turns out, was owned by a member of the Hell's Angels motorcycle gang. The man frequently brought his Harley-Davidson motorcycle inside during the winter and worked on its engine—which accounted for the traces of gasoline.

Many experts say that the most important thing about investigating a fire is to avoid giving in to the temptation of making assumptions before carefully looking at all the possibilities. "You can't have a preconceived notion of what happened," says Andy Vita of Alcohol, Tobacco and Firearms. "You have to let the evidence direct you to the solution."[15]

When all the evidence is weighed, and all accidental causes can be eliminated, then—and only then—the investigation quickly takes a new turn. The fire scene becomes a crime scene, and everything changes.

A Police Matter

The verdict that the fire is suspicious means that it is no longer merely a fire department matter, but one that involves the police department. "It's easier that way," says one police officer who has assisted on a number of arson cases. "Fire departments know

Investigators discuss clues they have found at a housing development that was set on fire near a nature preserve.

In 1996 a series of thirty church fires throughout the South led to both state and federal investigations.

everything about fighting fires, but they don't train their people to solve crimes. Police can get search warrants, do interviews, that kind of thing. So once we know that a fire is likely an arson, it becomes the domain of the police—usually police officers who specialize in investigating arson cases."[16]

As with any other crime, the purpose of an arson investigation is to discover not only the details of how the crime was committed, but also who committed the crime. To do that, it is necessary for the members of the arson squad to gather as much evidence as possible from the crime scene. Much of that evidence will be tested and examined in a crime laboratory.

Protecting the Crime Scene

Because it is crucial that the area be protected—either from curious onlookers or the arsonist hoping to remove incriminating evidence—a firefighter is left at the scene until all the investigative work is completed. There is another reason for a firefighter to remain at the scene, too, for once fire and investigative personnel have left the scene of a fire, they cannot resume their investigation without search warrants or the consent of the owner. Occasionally—especially if the owners themselves intentionally set the fire to defraud their insurance company, for example—they will be reluctant to allow further entrance to the scene.

"The law says we may be there for a reasonable length of time without warrants—a reasonable window of time to investigate how the fire started," explains McKenna. "'Reasonable' usually means enough time to get the smoke out of the structure, to allow time for the water to run off. But once you've disconnected the hoses and get out of there, it becomes more complicated for investigators. The aim is to get it done thoroughly and accurately while we've got a presence established there."[17]

With limited time, therefore, arson investigators and crime scene crews begin searching for answers to new questions. No longer is the issue "How did this fire start?" but "Who started this fire?" Every piece of information gathered at the scene, no matter how minuscule, may be the evidence that answers that question.

CHAPTER 2

Gathering Forensic Evidence

Two of the most important tools that help arson investigators do their job thoroughly and accurately are videotape and photography. Since the observations made by investigators, as well as the evidence collected at the scene, will likely be presented in court to a jury, it is crucial that the scene is documented completely—right from the beginning.

Documenting the Scene

Crime videographers need to view the outside of the structure as well as each room affected by the fire. It is especially important that the scene be reconstructed after the fire so that it resembles its original state as closely as possible and can be documented that way. This is no easy task, especially when fire damage is extensive; however, investigators find that seeing a room in its original state—especially the location of the point of origin—is invaluable in determining how the crime was committed.

That means dragging soggy, smoke-damaged sofas that firefighters removed while fighting the blaze back to a living room or ruined mattresses back into the bedroom. "We used to leave the fire scene cleaner than it was before the fire," says one former firefighter. "But after awhile, the lab guys told us to leave it, because it helped them when they worked the scene. We were destroying evidence without meaning to."[18]

Everything is documented and recorded—from a shot of the numbers showing the address of the structure to the condition of the point of origin of the fire. Crime photographers also take photographs of shoe prints in and around the building, along with photographs of the soles of shoes worn by

Arson investigators thoroughly document a fire scene with photographs and video.

police or firefighters. That way, they can eliminate prints made by those shoes as not belonging to the arsonist.

Looking for Accelerants

One of the first jobs for the crime lab crew is to search for evidence of any accelerant used. This is difficult for a number of reasons. First, accelerants such as kerosene, gasoline, or lighter fluid contain volatiles—the chemicals that make them flammable. These ingredients evaporate quickly; as one forensic scientist says, "Volatiles tend to walk away."[19] If investigators hope to find any traces of an accelerant at a fire scene, they must find them right away.

Another difficulty in finding traces of accelerant is that very little of it is needed to heighten a fire. With a large fire, it is extremely difficult to find the tiny traces that might (or might not) remain after the blaze has been put out. Accelerants adhere to the law of gravity, which means that they seep under carpets and into cracks in flooring—which makes it even harder to find traces of them.

Lab crews use various methods to look for accelerants. Some use a device called a hydrocarbon indicator, a portable instrument about the size of a

Matching Up Matches

Finding a match at a fire scene can be a lucky break. The torn edge of a match can lead investigators to the matchbook it came from and ultimately to a possible suspect. In David Fisher's Hard Evidence: How Detectives Inside the FBI's Sci-Crime Lab Have Helped Solve America's Toughest Cases, *forensic expert Jim Gerhardt explains how a match can be traced to a particular matchbook:*

"Turn a match on its side and you'll see little particles sticking out," he says. "Those particles will fit in perfectly with the adjoining matches in a matchbook, enabling us to make a microscopic comparison to prove that a match came from a specific matchbook to the exclusion of all other matchbooks ever made. I can often find as many as thirty different points of comparison in one match."

flashlight. As an investigator slowly walks through a fire scene with the indicator, any traces of an accelerant not burned by the flames will register positive on the dial. Explains one fire investigator, "It has a little vacuum in it that sucks in the vapors as you run it across the floor. It gives you a reading, and tells you if it's light or medium or heavy fuel [which would indicate the type of accelerant used]."[20]

Four-Legged Accelerant Detectors

Many arson experts favor the use of a different sort of accelerant indicator—an arson dog. More and more cities across the United States are using dogs to sniff out traces of hydrocarbons that sometimes even the most sophisticated electric sensors cannot find. In fact, these special dogs are able to detect traces of accelerant equal to .01 milliliter—or one-thousandth of a drop. In special tests by Alcohol, Tobacco and Firearms, the dogs had an accuracy rating of 100 percent.

The dogs are trained early in life to associate the smell of an accelerant like gasoline with a reward—usually praise or food from their handlers. Some trainers teach the dogs to sit when they detect an accelerant; others urge the dogs to paw at the area where they smell something. At first a few drops are hidden in a can, and the dogs have no trouble picking up the scent. Eventually, handlers introduce different accelerants, putting a drop or two under a rug or in a crack in cement. The results are amazing, say arson experts, largely because a dog's nose is more than 100,000 times more sensitive than a human nose. "A dog can go into a scene and within a minute or two, accurately pinpoint down to the size of a quarter flammable liquid or gasoline," says dog trainer Bill Whitstine. "The old way of investigating a small room—you might have to take fifteen or twenty samples and hope you get a sample [containing accelerant]."[21]

An arson dog handler in Oregon says that even after working for years with his dog, he is amazed at how the animal can make minuscule differentiations between accelerants and other chemical odors. "We train them [so that] if they're interested in an odor that's not an accelerant, they aren't rewarded. A lot of the scents are close—some items like polyurethane plastics and foam rubber cushions will change chemically in a fire, and the scents are almost identical to gas. Somehow the dog knows the difference—no one's sure how they do it."[22]

Being Careful

Once the presence of an accelerant has been detected, it is critically important for the evidence to be handled correctly. Because of the tendency of volatiles to evaporate when exposed to air, lab crews have to use particular care.

"We use clean paint cans for samples containing accelerants and other volatiles," says forensic chemist Dave Tebow of Minnesota's State Bureau of Criminal Apprehension (BCA). "Not a plastic bag—the plastic can react chemically with the hydrocarbons in the sample. When that happens the plastic bag would become damaged, giving the volatiles a way to escape.

"These paint cans we use are lined with an epoxy resin that doesn't contaminate the sample, yet it seals it in. The lining is virtually indestructible—I've taken a blowtorch to resins, and they don't break down. Anyway, each sample—whether from a floorboard, a piece of linoleum, whatever—is put in one of the cans."[23]

Arson investigators also say that it is important to take unburned sections of carpet or flooring, too. Many carpets, linoleums, and adhesives used in tile contain volatile hydrocarbons that might be mistaken for accelerant in the lab. By having a comparison sample, the crime lab can be more accurate in determining the type of accelerant that was used in an arson fire.

Time-Delay Devices

The crime scene processors do not confine their work to searching for accelerants. Other kinds of evidence at a crime scene can be valuable to investigators, too. Many times, evidence of

Arson dogs use their acute sense of smell to sniff out possible accelerants.

A close examination of evidence can often indicate whether a fire was caused by arson or accident.

a timing device can be found in the fire debris. A timing device is an ignition method that allows arsonists to get away from the scene by the time the fire starts. This enables the arsonists to have an alibi for their whereabouts at the time of the fire and also lets them avoid the danger of being caught in the fire they set.

There are many ways to delay the start of an arson fire. "You see candles a lot," says McKenna. "Somebody lights a candle, sprinkles some accelerant on some paper, puts it at the base of the candle. With an average-size candle, like you'd use on a dinner table, for instance, you'd get at least a half-hour before the candle burned down enough to ignite the paper."[24]

Occasionally, an arsonist tries to make the fire look accidental by tampering with an appliance such as an electric coffeepot or slow cooker. "These sorts of appliances have a thermal fuse, which prevents it from overheating," explains Dave Tebow. "At a certain temperature, the fuse blows. But what an arsonist might do is remove the fuse and rewire the appliance without it. They might put an accelerant in it, maybe some paper around the base of the appliance, and they have time to get out before it ignites—anywhere from a few minutes to a half hour."[25]

Anything that could have been used as a time-delay device is photographed where it was found, labeled, and put into a separate container or bag. Later, the evidence is examined more thoroughly to learn whether it was used to commit the crime. A suspicious coffeepot, for example, will be X-rayed to see if its fuse has been tampered with.

Picking Up the Trash

Time-delay devices are not the only items taken to the lab for analysis. Anything found at the scene that might yield a clue to the arsonist's identity is removed. Trash in and around the fire scene is collected—everything from candy wrappers and soda cans to broken glass and tiny pieces of paper. After everything visible in or near the house is examined, crime scene crews process any evidence that might be found under the surface of the debris.

"Almost anything you find could help the investigators later," says Steve Banning, a crime lab specialist. "The fire scene may be a complete disaster, but you treat it like an archaeological dig. We go through the ashes, the debris, with little sifters, you know, looking for the tiniest details.

"It's slow work—in a crime scene I worked recently, a two-story house had burned completely, down to the ground. Everything was down in the basement—nothing of the structure left. But you go through all that ash, and you find things. A button, a matchbook, a cartridge, anything that might help later you put aside, and later it will be examined for fingerprints. Of course, most of what you find won't be

Arson investigators carefully search through every piece of trash and debris.

The Father of Forensic Science

Edmond Locard, a French police detective in the late nineteenth and early twentieth centuries, developed the idea that when a person visits a location, he or she leaves behind trace evidence—usually so tiny and insignificant as to go unnoticed—and takes evidence away as well. A few cat hairs clinging to a murderer's coat, for example, might be left behind at the murder scene. At the same time, threads from the victim's carpet might be embedded in the murderer's shoes.

Locard's idea, known today as Locard's Exchange Principle, has become the basis of much forensic science. Because of Locard, crime scenes today are secured until technicians can painstakingly gather any dirt, threads, hairs, or other trace evidence that might prove helpful in an investigation.

relevant, but you can't discount anything while you're doing it. You never know what could be the thing that ties the whole case together for the investigators."[26]

Expanding the Investigators' View

Until recently, arson investigators limited their work to finding traces of accelerant and ignition or time-delay devices. However, Banning says, forensic scientists are urging them to remember that a suspicious fire scene is also a crime scene. "You can do a lot more than just process accelerants," he says. "We want to get arson investigators to widen their view a little. If it was an arson fire, that means that the arsonist had to have been there on the premises at some time. That means that some trace of him has been left there."[27]

Like other forensic scientists, Banning believes in the principle espoused by French scientist Edmond Locard. Locard's Exchange Principle, as it is known, says that whenever two bodies come into contact, each leaves something behind—whether something obvious and easy to see, such as a dropped glove, or something minuscule, like a hair or fingerprint.

"That is the basis of what we do—look for the traces. Of course, the fire scene is the worst place to do that," Banning acknowledges. "Hair, fibers, all kinds of the tiniest traces of evidence are not easy to find at a fire scene, as they are at a homicide, for example. But the fact is, traces are there—the arsonist leaves something behind. It's up to us to find it, that's all."[28]

Tire Treads

One bit of evidence often left behind at fire scenes is tire tracks. Investigators pay particular attention to any tread marks near

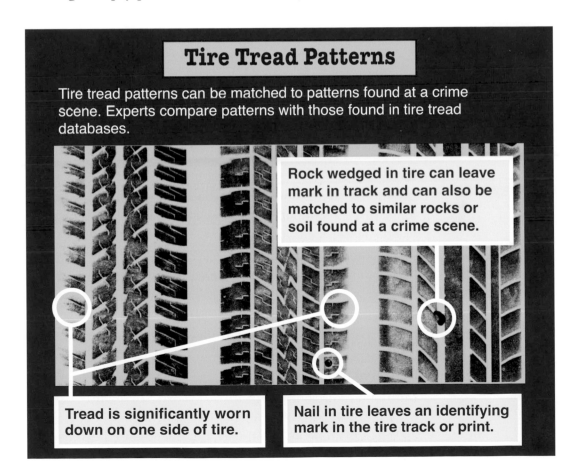

Tire Tread Patterns

Tire tread patterns can be matched to patterns found at a crime scene. Experts compare patterns with those found in tire tread databases.

Rock wedged in tire can leave mark in track and can also be matched to similar rocks or soil found at a crime scene.

Tread is significantly worn down on one side of tire.

Nail in tire leaves an identifying mark in the tire track or print.

the fire scene, for they could provide some clue about the vehicle driven by the arsonist. Since each type of tire leaves a different pattern, the treads can easily point to the manufacturer and model of the tire.

If the vehicle has been driven through paint, tar, or some other substance easy to see, traces of it might be visible on concrete or hard asphalt. Crime scene crews can even find latent, or hidden, tread marks. Investigators take extensive photographs of the marks, and in the lab, technicians can often identify the brand of tire by comparing these marks with samples from various tire models.

Lots to Learn from a Shoe Pattern

Shoe prints around the fire scene are treated as possible evidence, too. Shoe prints can provide clues that are even more helpful than tire tracks. Not only can a database on a lab computer identify the brand of virtually any shoe by the pattern of the sole, but an examination of the shoe print can provide information about how a person walks. Does the shoe's wearer step with the heels down first or walk on the balls of the feet? These characteristics are reflected in how the sole is worn down. Does the person limp? In a three-dimensional view of the prints, one shoe print will be deeper than the other.

Tire tracks can provide clues about an arsonist's car.

According to forensic expert D.P. Lyle, shoes can even give clues as to the type of work a person does. "From one day to the next, people routinely walk over the same kinds of surfaces during the normal course of their activities; however, the types of surfaces they walk on vary from person to person. As a result, the wear patterns on the soles of the shoes of an office worker who walks across carpets most of the day vary greatly from those of a construction worker who frequently stomps through gravel or across rough concrete."[29]

Shoe prints, like tire tracks, are documented extensively with photographs. If tread marks or shoe prints are in some soft material, such as clay or mud, the crime scene crews use an additional method to process them. After photographing the impression, they make a casting of it using plaster. The technician places a metal or wood frame around the tire or shoe print, then pours plaster into the impression and allows it to set before removing it. Plaster casts are put into cardboard boxes and taken to the crime lab for analysis.

 ## Making an Impression of a Shoe Print

1 **The tread mark** is photographed against a bright light source that can show the depth of the mark as well as any small abnormalities in the tread, such as unusually worn areas or nicks or gouges in the sole of the shoe.

2 **A metal or wooden frame** is placed around the mark.

3 **A quick-drying, hard type of plaster** is poured into the impression and allowed to set. The forensic technician usually scratches the date and his or her initials into the plaster cast before the cast hardens completely. This information removes any doubt later in court as to when and by whom the impression was made.

4 **The hardened cast** is placed into a cardboard box and sealed, so it can be stored as evidence in a secure location until it is needed in court.

Snow Prints

Shoe prints and tire treads in snow present a special problem, since snow is so unstable. As the sun warms the surface of the snow print, it can melt quickly. As it melts, details in the original impression shift and change. And because it is such a fragile impression, pouring a heavy plaster mixture on it would destroy it. Instead, forensic crews use hot sulfur.

"I know it sounds odd," says one BCA scientist:

> You normally wouldn't pour something hot on snow, but sulfur is endothermic, which means that it doesn't give off heat. You can get it to a liquid and it starts to form crystals; then you can pour it into the footprint, tire track, whatever. It forms a very nice image. It's hard, like plaster, but a little more fragile. There's also a product called Snow Print Wax, which you can apply to the print, like spray paint. It gives it a little shell, and afterwards you can safely use a plaster cast. Snow print impressions, like other track impressions, are put in a cardboard box and sent to the lab.[30]

The ability to make permanent impressions of shoe prints at a fire scene has sometimes given investigators the evidence they needed to make an arrest. In one case, a winter fire destroyed a young man's home. There were shoe prints near the scene, but they were unusual. "They were footprints, but every so often, there would be a little round mark on one side," Tebow explains:

> They made the sulfur casts of it all—and eventually they looked at what they had, and realized the little hole was a cane mark. The prints belonged to a neighbor—a man whose daughter was dating the victim. The [neighbor] was angry because [the victim] had been abusive towards his daughter—so he burned the guy's house down. At first, he had denied being anywhere

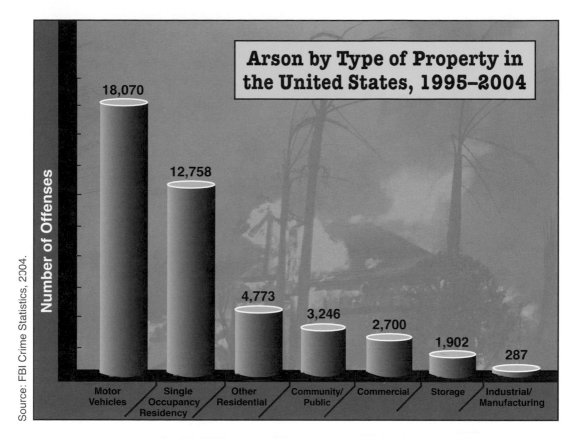

Arson by Type of Property in the United States, 1995–2004

Number of Offenses

Source: FBI Crime Statistics, 2004.

18,070 — Motor Vehicles
12,758 — Single Occupancy Residency
4,773 — Other Residential
3,246 — Community/Public
2,700 — Commercial
1,902 — Storage
287 — Industrial/Manufacturing

near the scene, but because of the recent snow, and the cane marks, he was clearly lying. They solved that case because of the snowprint.[31]

All Kinds of Evidence

Tire tracks and shoe prints are not the only kinds of evidence that investigators may use to solve an arson case. Almost anything, however seemingly unimportant, can eventually point to a particular suspect. For example, at one fire scene investigators found the tip of a screwdriver on the ground. It was photographed and removed from the scene as evidence—although they had nothing to tie it to any certain person. Later, however, when a suspect was found, police discovered a broken screwdriver in the backseat of his car. At the lab, scientists saw

The tools an arsonist uses to gain entry to a building may leave telltale marks behind.

that the two parts matched up perfectly. "The guy had claimed he was in another state on that night," recalls one police officer. "But that screwdriver placed him there, so it showed he was not being truthful with the police."[32]

"You Just Never Know"

Arsonists may use tools such as screwdrivers to gain entry to a structure by prying open a door or window. In such cases, scratches or gouges made by the tool can provide evidence that can be helpful to investigators. Common tools may all look the same, but each one has imperfections that make the marks it leaves unique.

Investigators make casts of tool marks just as they do tire treads or shoe prints. If an arson suspect is identified and a tool found that may have made the marks, these casts can provide a basis for comparison. In the lab, technicians use the suspect's tool to make a mark in some soft surface, such as clay or putty. This ensures that the blade is not damaged during the laboratory test, thus making the results questionable. After making a mark with the tool, the technician uses a comparison microscope to examine both marks—the one left at the scene and the sample made in the lab. If they are similar, it is likely that they were made by the same tool.

Tool marks are but one type of evidence that can solve an arson case. "You never know what sort of break you'll get from evidence you find at the scene," Steve Banning says. "Sometimes it seems like something so insignificant, like you're just collecting a bunch of stuff that means nothing—you don't even know if it has to do with the crime or if it's just trash. But later, it might be just the thing you need. You just never know."[33]

CHAPTER 3

Analyzing the Evidence

Once the evidence from the fire scene is taken to the crime lab, it must be tested and evaluated to extract every possible bit of information. Such evidence may not only point to the arsonist, but also exonerate a suspect who is innocent. Because the stakes are so high, it is crucial for forensic scientists to be accurate and thorough. Notes one laboratory technician, "You understand while you're working that people's lives—their reputations, whether or not they get arrested and go to jail—everything hangs in the balance. It's an awesome responsibility."[34]

"Bad Guys Are Usually Not That Smart"

Once the collected evidence is back at the crime lab, it is assigned to various technicians for analysis. Any items that may have fingerprints on them are carefully examined. A beer can or even a bag containing potato chip crumbs found near the scene might have been left by the arsonist, so technicians test such things for fingerprints.

"Same with a container that might have been used to transport an accelerant, a screwdriver or crowbar that might have been used to gain illegal entry into a structure, a partial book of matches, or even a single match," says police officer Sean McKenna. "You never know what the guys in the lab will get. On television, of course, the bad guys always protect their identity by wearing gloves, but in real life bad guys are usually not that smart."[35]

Some fingerprints are easy to see. A person who has touched blood or paint, for example, will leave behind prints. These are called patent fingerprints. Plastic prints are obvious,

A laboratory technician records evidence analysis results at FBI headquarters in Washington, D.C.

Latent Fingerprints

Exposing the fingerprints to a special light will sometimes cause the prints to appear.

A soft brush is used to dust a fine, colored powder over the surface of the evidence. The powder sticks to the latent prints.

too. These are three-dimensional prints that occur if a person's finger has left an impression on a soft surface, such as dust, wax, or putty. Both plastic and patent fingerprints can be photographed at the scene, although at fire scenes—because of the likelihood of exposure to weather if the fire was very destructive—items with such fingerprints are often brought to the crime lab to be photographed.

Most of the time, however, the fingerprints at a crime scene are neither plastic or patent. Instead, they are latent, or invisible, created by the tiny ridges on the inner surfaces of the tips of one's fingers. These ridges are lined with pores that allow sweat to leave the body. The ridges also pick up traces of sweat from touching the face and other parts of the body. It is the pattern of moisture left by the ridges on fingertips that makes up a latent fingerprint. Fingerprint experts use chemicals that can highlight latent fingerprints so they can be photographed and their images taken back to the crime lab.

Latent fingerprints are not visible to the naked eye. Depending on the object and quality of the prints, forensic technicians use different methods to locate and preserve latent prints.

The dusted print is covered with clear, sticky tape and carefully lifted off. The tape is placed on a plastic card for later comparison.

Instead of dust, steam from an iron is sometimes applied to porous materials like paper and cardboard to bring prints into view.

AFIS

When a fingerprint is recovered from an arson scene, it is compared to the fingerprints of anyone who normally had access to that scene. In the case of a house fire, for instance, investigators would check that fingerprint against those of the occupants, their friends, babysitters—anyone whose fingerprints would normally be there. These prints are called elimination prints. If a fingerprint does not match any of those, and if investigators are certain that the arsonist is not one of those people, it is likely that it belongs to the individual who started the fire.

At the crime lab, suspicious fingerprints are routinely run through a computerized fingerprint database called the Automatic Fingerprint Identification System, or AFIS. AFIS, which is maintained by the Federal Bureau of Investigation, contains the fingerprints of more than 44 million people with criminal records in the United States. AFIS is constantly updated as new people enter into the criminal justice system.

Becoming a Fingerprint Examiner

Job Description:

The latent print examiner processes evidence, looking for latent fingerprints; recovers latent prints with a variety of chemicals; and photographs and makes copies of each print to be used as evidence in the investigation. In addition, the examiner is responsible for entering the data into the AFIS system, so it can be compared to fingerprints already on file.

A fingerprint examiner runs suspicious fingerprints through the AFIS database.

Education:

Each city or county has its own requirements, but most expect an examiner to have completed at least two years of college and to have advanced certification showing that the applicant has mastered a specialized course of study of fingerprint analysis.

Qualifications:

Complete knowledge of the variety of chemicals, powders, and alternative light sources used in processing latent prints. In addition, the applicant must understand federal, state, and local laws and codes concerning the gathering of fingerprint evidence.

Salary:

An entry-level latent print examiner usually earns an annual salary ranging from $42,000 to $58,000.

Using the System

The AFIS system does not actually scan entire fingerprints, but rather searches for key points of comparison. A technician chooses specific characteristics in the fingerprint that can be used to search the AFIS database.

"For instance, you identify certain bifurcations, which are the Y-shaped ridges on a fingerprint, or perhaps an island [a mark that is not connected to ridges] or something like that," explains Dave Tebow, a forensics expert:

> You mark certain specific points for the computer to search. Often, too, the examiner in the lab may limit the computer search to a particular area, so you're not checking the print against their entire database for the whole country.
>
> You start out with the most likely, which usually would be someone local—at least in an arson case. If an arson took place in, say, Wisconsin, you'd narrow down to a subset of the database that includes Wisconsin, Iowa, North and South Dakota, and Minnesota. That will take less time than searching a larger area. And if that doesn't work, you can always go bigger.[36]

AFIS usually comes up with several possible matches—fingerprints in its database that share the same individual points of comparison marked by the examiner. That examiner will then use a special magnifying glass to look at each print, hoping to find one that not only shares those certain characteristics, but is an exact match.

Solving a Case

The identification of a latent fingerprint on an ignition device was credited with the arrest of a serial arsonist operating in California during the late 1980s and 1990s. The arsonist is

believed by some experts to have set two thousand fires over a ten-year period—including fires in homes and businesses, as well as brush fires.

At one scene, an ignition device was discovered before it had a chance to go off. The device was simple—a cigarette and three paper matches wrapped loosely in a piece of yellow notepaper. The paper was sent to the lab, where it was bathed in a chemical called ninhydrin. A very clear purplish fingerprint appeared on the paper.

When the print was first run, there was no computer database for fingerprints. Although investigators did not yet have a suspect, they saved the print, hoping that if they ever had a suspect, they could get a match between that individual's print and the one from the timing device. Years later, when a similar timing device was found at a nearby arson fire, the fingerprint was finally identified—and the results stunned everyone.

The print belonged to an arson investigator named John Orr, one of the most highly recognized firefighters in California. At first investigators thought that Orr's print ended up on the ignition device because he had been assisting on the case. Arson investigator Mike Matassa recalls that a lab examiner called him after the lab identified the print. "He says, 'We got a hit—but it's one of your investigators.' We said, 'What are you talking about?' He says, 'John Orr. He should know enough not to handle the evidence. Tell that dummy not to handle the evidence.'"

However, Matassa and his staff knew that Orr had not assisted with this case. "Everybody's jaw dropped with that remark, because there's no reason John Orr should have been involved anywhere in an investigation in Bakersfield, when he's in Glendale . . . it was like we couldn't believe it."[37] As the investigation progressed, however, the team realized that Orr had indeed been involved. His fingerprint on the incendiary device was the evidence investigators needed to prove it.

Tight Seals Are Critical

While some of the crime lab technicians deal with fingerprints recovered from the scene, others verify the presence of an accelerant. Even if arson dogs reacted strongly to a smell at the scene, it must be scientifically documented. No matter how sensitive an arson dog's nose is, says one lawyer who specializes in arson cases, the dog's reaction to a smell at a fire scene will not stand up without verification. "As far as I know," he says, "a dog's never been able to testify in court that he smelled gasoline [at the fire scene]. It's the laboratory that's got to show proof."[38]

To do this, crime scene crews put pieces of flooring, upholstery, or carpet in clean, tightly sealed paint cans. Larger items such as sofas may be tightly wrapped in sheets of a specially formulated nylon/polyester blend. Either way, the goal is the same: to prevent vapors from evaporating before the samples reach the lab. "We worked a case once where the police department submitted several pieces of burned wood recovered from a suspicious fire in a bar," says forensic specialist John Houde. "They had carefully packaged the wood in paper sacks, just like we train them to do—for

Former arson investigator John Orr was convicted of twenty counts of arson in 1998.

blood evidence! Two months later they asked us to check the wood for traces of gasoline. The tests all came up negative. Small wonder."[39]

Headspace and Charcoal Strips

When picking up these samples, crime scene crews are careful not to fill the cans to the brim with evidence. Instead, they leave several inches of what is called "headspace" at the top of the can. Vapors rise, and headspace gives them room to do so. When the lid is taken off the can at the lab, a strip of plastic coated with charcoal is quickly inserted into the headspace.

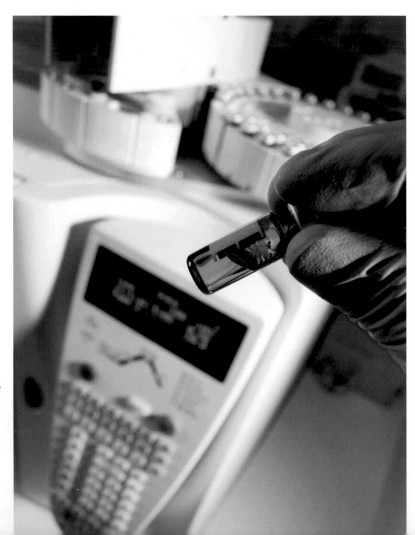

Gas chromatograph machines are used to test samples collected at a fire scene for the presence of hydrocarbons, a sign of accelerant use.

Looking for Suspicious Chemicals

Investigators use the GC/MS test to look for suspicious chemicals that might have been used to start a fire. The test works this way:

1 **The chemical or other element** suspected of containing an accelerant such as gasoline, lighter fluid, or kerosene is injected into one end of a column.

2 **The column** is heated, which changes the sample from a liquid into a gas.

3 **Helium,** an inert gas, is forced through the column, carrying the gas sample with it but not reacting with it. Each ingredient in the sample travels through the column at a different rate, since each has a different weight, so the ingredients are separated from one another.

4 **Each ingredient** is then bombarded with an electron stream, which breaks it into fragments and molecules.

5 **The fragments** are passed through a magnetic field that filters and separates them.

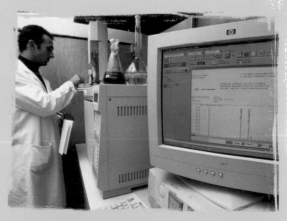

6 **A computer** attached to the instrument calculates the molecular mass of each fragment and identifies the ingredients based on their molecular formulas. The computer produces a graph of these data, which can be read by the instrument operator.

A forensic scientist prepares a sample for chemical analysis.

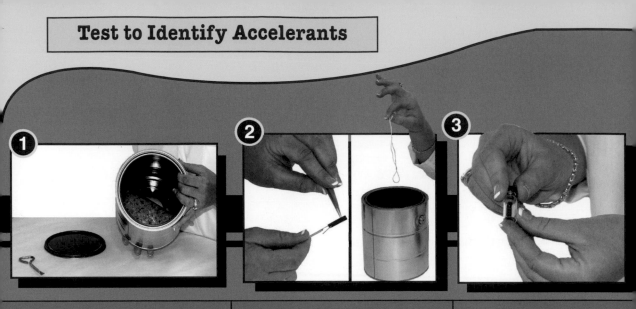

Test to Identify Accelerants

1 Arson investigators place evidence such as carpet or clothing fibers in a clean paint can, then seal the can, and deliver it to crime lab technicians.

2 Lab technicians open the can and insert a strip of carbon. The carbon is attached to a paper clip and suspended from a piece of dental floss. The can is then resealed and heated.

3 After about 2 hours at 176°F, the carbon strip has absorbed some of the accelerant. It is removed from the can and placed in a vial with liquid solvent.

Charcoal acts as a magnet, absorbing any hydrocarbons, which are present in all accelerants. Each can is prepared the same way.

To speed up the process of vapors rising, the can is resealed and warmed in a lab oven for several hours. After the can is removed from the oven, the technician removes the strip and places it in a solution that removes the hydrocarbons from the charcoal strip. A small amount of this liquid is then injected into a machine called a gas chromatograph, or GC, for analysis.

The GC is one of the most valuable tools in the crime lab because it is able to detect various components of a sample. In arson cases, investigators need to find out if there are any traces of accelerants in the solution made from the charcoal-covered strip hanging in the sample from the fire scene. In some cases, the GC is used to tell whether a sample of blood found at a crime scene contains an illegal drug or a poison.

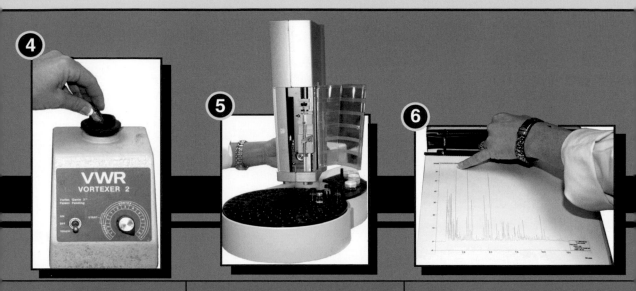

4 The vial is then inserted in a Vortexer, where some of the accelerant from the carbon strip is deposited into the liquid solvent.

5 A gas chromatograph heats the liquid until it becomes gas. The various components of the gas travel through a long column at different rates. The rates are recorded on a graph.

6 The graph pattern identifies the accelerant as light, such as charcoal lighter fluid or gasoline; medium, such as mineral spirits; or heavy, such as kerosene or jet fuel.

The GC and the Mass Spec

The first step in GC analysis is to inject the liquid solution made from the vapors into the front of the GC. The device immediately heats the sample, changing it back into a gas. The sample is then swept into a long tube.

Each component present in the sample passes through the tube at a different rate, depending on its chemical makeup. A computer attached to the GC measures the speed at which each component travels through the tube, and creates a chart with peaks and valleys that resembles the printout of a lie detector test. Each peak and valley represents one component in the solution.

The gas chromatograph is frequently connected to another machine called a mass spectrometer, or mass spec. As each component comes out of the GC, it is separate from the others, in a pure form. The mass spec bombards each component with a stream of tiny particles called electrons. That breaks the component into fragments. Says forensic expert Dave

Tebow, "We take that pattern of fragmentation, and we can identify exactly what that component is."[40]

The pattern produced by the mass spec can be run through the lab's database and matched with a high degree of accuracy to a component. "We have access to a library of more than 3 million components," says Tebow. "Our own lab has 265 compounds that are related just to arson cases. It's not just accelerants, either. We have patterns of components that are found on new carpeting. And if we're running an analysis of clothing from a person in a fire, we can identify tiny substances that make up human sweat, too. If it's there, we can identify it."[41]

Researchers use mass spectrometers along with gas chromatography to examine the chemical composition of material samples from fire scenes.

Case Solved

Tebow says that a GC/mass spec profile of an accelerant was crucial evidence that led to an arrest in a 1999 arson case in Minnesota. "We had a fire, and at the scene they found a pop can, a candy wrapper, a gas can, and of course, the traces of gas used in the fire. The pop can and candy wrapper were outside, but still within the yellow crime

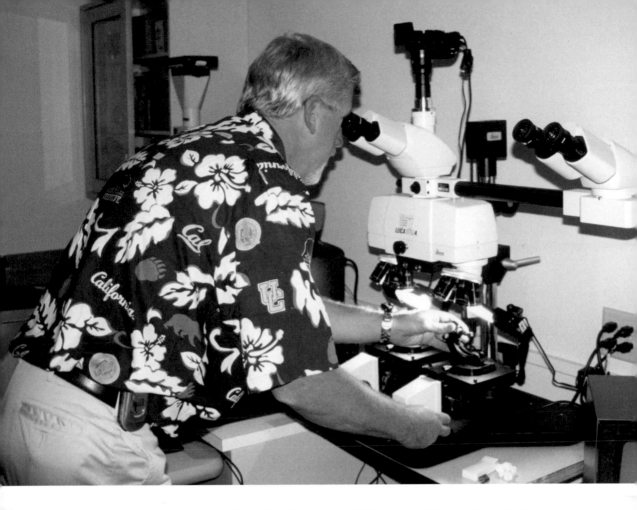

scene tape, so we processed it, hoping it would be helpful to the case."

Fingerprints taken from the soda can and the candy wrapper yielded no computer matches. The case seemed stalled until the lab ran the accelerant through the GC/mass spec. "What it showed was gasoline with almost no sulfur, very low alkanes [a type of hydrocarbon]," Tebow says. "We have a gas refinery here that makes a product called Blue Planet, which I think is the only gasoline that has already met the environmental standards for 2010—really low sulfur and a very low alkane reading, too. I told the investigator that I was reasonably confident that the gasoline used came from a Holiday station—those are the ones that sell that gasoline."

Investigators found that there was a Holiday station only a few blocks from the fire scene. "They went with the assumption

A special microscope allows forensic scientists to compare tool marks left at a crime scene with those made by a tool belonging to a suspect.

that people don't usually drive for miles with a gas can in their car," says Tebow. "It's possible, yes, but not as likely. So the investigators went to that station, and pulled the surveillance tapes from the day of the fire. And there they were—two juveniles, buying a gas can, pop, candy, and gas. So [the investigators] had a visual identification of the suspects. They were picked up for questioning, and that was it."[42]

Unique Defects

While traces of an accelerant can be valuable evidence, the crime lab can also learn a great deal about criminals by the tool marks they leave at the scene. Crime scene crews bring in any items damaged by chisels, wrenches, or crowbars, and these are examined under a microscope.

Tools, no matter how similar they look to the naked eye, are in reality quite different. Every tool has blemishes, nicks, gouges, and other imperfections that can be seen under a microscope. Some of these marks are created during the manufacturing process, while others are a result of normal wear. The forensic scientist checks the marks left by the tool and notes the imperfections. When arson investigators have a suspect, they search that person's home, garage, and vehicles for tools that might have made the marks.

In the lab, the suspect tool is used to make a mark on a surface much like the one already in evidence. Afterwards, a technician looks at the two marks side by side, using a special instrument called a comparison microscope. This microscope consists of two regular microscopes that are combined with prisms that can bring two images side by side for direct comparison. By looking at the original tool mark side by side with the one made in the lab, a forensic scientist can say with certainty whether the two were made by the suspect tool.

Manufacturing imperfections found on tools create marks that can be used like fingerprints to track down an arsonist.

A Bubble as Evidence

Arson investigators say that it is not unusual for a tool mark to play an important role in an investigation. "I worked a case several years ago where someone set fire to a clothing store," says Dale, a police officer:

> There was no doubt it was an arson, and the fire marshals got the police in there right away. The arsonist had gotten in by using bolt cutters on a thick chain that was on the back of the building, near the loading dock door.
>
> They sent the chain to the lab, and they found there was a defect in the bolt cutters—one of the blades had an air bubble in it or something—you could see it real clear under a microscope, but the guy probably didn't notice. The lab told us it was something that happened when the tool was made.

Dale says that an employee who had been recently fired had made threats against the store owners, and someone had tipped the store owner that the employee might try something to get even. "We had a warrant, and we found bolt cutters in the trunk of his car. The lab did a comparison, and the mark was the same—the air bubble in the exact same spot. It was a great piece of evidence for us. You hear this time and time again, but it's true—the littlest, least likely things trip criminals up. I mean, an air bubble? Who would ever think of that?"[43]

CHAPTER 4

Investigating Fatal Fires

While the crime lab's work is important in examining any suspicious fire, it is especially critical when there are fatalities involved. Dr. Michael McGee, a medical examiner, says that there is always a special urgency about a fire death when arson is suspected.

"A Whole Different Thing"

"We had a death a few years ago. A fire started on the front porch of a house and spread to the upstairs," he recalls:

> Anyway, one little boy escaped from upstairs, but there were three or four brothers and sisters, and they couldn't get out—they all died. The fire department decided quickly that it was a suspicious fire. Something like that, just the suspicious nature of it, you're going to treat it differently than a case of someone found dead in a house fire, where a wood stove was burning. While any fire death is a crisis, an arson death is a whole different thing.[44]

McGee and other medical examiners are called in when a death is believed to be suspicious. Most medical examiners are trained as forensic pathologists, which means they are investigators of a sort; they are looking for clues that tell how the person died. However, the evidence they examine is not the crime scene, but rather the body of the victim. Using the crime lab, medical examiners perform autopsies—postmortem examinations—on fire victims to gather every sort of information they can from the bodies.

A fire that involves human fatalities requires arson investigators and medical examiners to collaborate during the investigation.

"What gives the job urgency is that police cannot go forward with their job—solving the crime—until they know why that person died," McGee explains. "Was the cause smoke inhalation, or a heart attack? Or was that person stabbed or shot? And what about the manner of death? Was there a suicide? Was the death an accident, or was it a homicide? These are things police investigators need to know before they can begin their investigation."[45]

In the meantime, however, the medical examiner treats the body as if the crime were a homicide. The clothes are carefully examined for trace evidence—blood, hairs, fibers—that may be important later in establishing who was responsible for the death.

Identifying the Victim

Fire deaths can be particularly challenging, for many bodies are burned to such an extent that identification is difficult. In some cases, determining the sex or race of the body is impossible without some outside information.

"Normally, with many deaths, you can have a family member identify the victim with a photograph, or they can come in to view the body," says McGee. "But obviously, in crimes like arson, or when there is an explosion or something—when the body is so badly burned, you have to do something different.

"This is why medical investigation at the scene depends a great deal on police," he continues:

> Even at a residential fire, where you think it would be pretty easy to narrow down who the victim might be, you want information from the police. You can't necessarily assume anything. If it's the Johnsons' house— maybe they're a normal family, you know. Maybe they're not. Maybe the home is being rented by someone. Maybe *they're* normal people, maybe they're not. Maybe the house is being used as a meth lab. See? We have to have a vague idea before we start, before we even open the bag.[46]

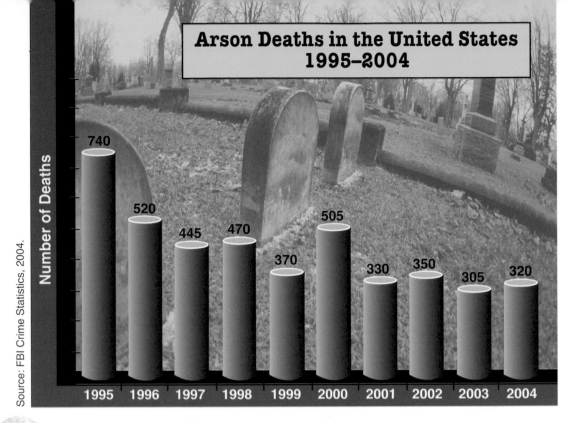

Arson Deaths in the United States 1995–2004

Number of Deaths

Source: FBI Crime Statistics, 2004.

- 1995: 740
- 1996: 520
- 1997: 445
- 1998: 470
- 1999: 370
- 2000: 505
- 2001: 330
- 2002: 350
- 2003: 305
- 2004: 320

The Gold Standard of Identification

In past generations, fingerprints were considered the best way of getting an accurate identification of a body. However, in fire deaths, the outer layer of skin on the fingers is often burned so badly that no fingerprint can be taken. And even if a print can be made, says McGee, most people have not been fingerprinted.

"Unless you are a police officer, or are in the security business," he explains, "or you have served in the armed forces, or you have a criminal record, you haven't got fingerprints on file. So even if [investigators are] lucky enough to get a clear fingerprint from a body, running it through the database, [they will] never get a match, never find out who it belongs to."

Modern forensic scientists consider dental identification to be the most reliable method of body identification. "By today's standards, dental ID is the gold standard," says McGee. "Unlike fingerprints, most people *have* gone to dentists; they have had teeth filled or X-rayed. So we are far more likely to be successful in examining the teeth to learn someone's identity."[47]

Looking at the Teeth

Besides, says one fire investigator, teeth and bones are more likely to survive fires than the skin on fingers. "It's lucky for the crime lab," he acknowledges:

> Especially in cases where you get a person who sets a fire as really an afterthought. It happens more than people might realize—somebody kills somebody, and they set the place on fire to cover the crime. But it's really, really hard to completely destroy a body by burning.

Medical examiners often use dental X-rays to identify fire victims.

> [Some criminals] think they can burn down the crime scene, and all the evidence will be gone, but that isn't the case. Truthfully, I've never had a case where a fire has totally consumed the body—never. There's always something left. Even in a crematorium, where the fires are like 2,000° [F; 1,093°C] and burn for hours and hours, you still get teeth and bone fragments—and arson fires almost never get that hot.[48]

In the lab, a forensic dentist takes dental X-rays and removes the upper and lower jaws so that the teeth can be carefully charted. The dentist looks not only at the fillings in the teeth, but also at crowns, evidence of root canal surgery, and even the spacing between teeth. Once the teeth have been charted, the forensic dentist compares the chart to the dental records of likely victims of the fire.

In the case of a fire in a house or an office where only a limited number of known people could be the fire victim, investigators simply find out from friends or family who that person's dentist is and procure the dental X-rays from that dentist. Even in cases where not all the teeth survive a fire, it is surprising how helpful teeth can be to forensic scientists.

Even a Single Tooth

In one highly publicized case in 1999, a man abducted and murdered nineteen-year-old Katie Poirier, who had been working at a convenience store in rural Minnesota. When burned human remains were found in a firepit on the man's property, police thought the remains could be those of the missing young woman.

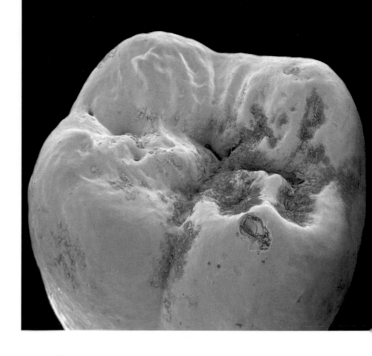

Teeth can have unique features that help forensics dentists match records with victims.

The fire damage to the body was so extensive that there was no hope of testing DNA. In fact, all that crime lab crews found were a few charred bones and a single tooth. Amazingly, it was the tooth that made all the difference to the investigation.

Just ten days before she was abducted, Poirier had had dental work done on her lower left molar, which was the same tooth found in the firepit. Her dentist had replaced an old filling, using a sample of a new dental adhesive she had received at a dentists' convention. The new product contained a substance called zirconium, and at the time, the adhesive was the only product on the market with that ingredient.

Using the Electron Microscope

The forensic lab examined the tooth and found that it had traces of a filling. They looked at part of the filling using a scanning electron microscope, or SEM. Unlike most other microscopes, which use light to focus on an object, the SEM works by scanning a beam of electrons over an object. As the beam sweeps across, it provides a greatly magnified, clear image of even the tiniest bits of evidence. The beam also causes the substance being examined to release energy as X-rays. Because different substances give off these rays in characteristic wavelengths, analyzing the X-ray spectrum can tell investigators what the substance is composed of.

When investigators used SEM X-ray analysis to examine the material from Poirier's tooth, it identified traces of zirconium. Because the zirconium adhesive was so rare, medical investigators were confident that the tooth and other remains were those of Poirier. Says one police officer, "It's incredibly hard to imagine the odds of finding that particular tooth which was so unique—that really provided the positive ID the police and Katie's family were looking for."[49]

When Dental Identification Is Unlikely

When police have no idea of the identity of a burned body—or part of a body—dental X-rays are not helpful, since there is no way of knowing the victim's dentist and thereby obtaining dental records. In such cases, forensic pathologists can try to take fingerprints that they can at least run through the fingerprint database, AFIS.

"You might have a fire in an abandoned building," says one lab technician, "or in a commercial structure where it is almost impossible to come up with likely names for victims. In an old abandoned warehouse or something, you are likely to see homeless people.

"There was a case in Detroit in 2001 where an abandoned building burned and there were a number of fatalities—most of them homeless people who'd been on the street for years and years," she continues. "Not much chance of an ID with dental X-rays, since most hadn't seen the inside of a dentist's office. I know that the medical examiner up there was able to get fingerprints . . . and at least two of [the people] had been through the [criminal justice] system, so their prints were on file."[50]

Unusual Fingerprint Methods

Fingerprinting a burned body can be very difficult, but in cases such as this one, forensic pathologists employ some unusual techniques. For instance, in cases where the intense heat of a fire has shriveled the skin on the fingers, a saline solution known as tissue builder is injected into the fingertips. Tissue builder causes the fingertips to swell to a more normal shape that can be fingerprinted.

In cases where the epidermis, or outer layer of skin, is so charred that the fingerprint ridges cannot be seen, it can be cut away by the medical examiner and prints can be obtained from the second layer of skin.

"If [the second layer] is intact but too soft or flabby to be printed," says researcher David Fisher, "it can be sliced off, and after being briefly bathed in alcohol, slipped over the specialist's own finger, and printed as if it were part of that finger."[51] Sometimes, too, the ridge detail cannot be seen on the outside of the finger, but is still visible on the inner side. In that case, a forensic pathologist can turn the skin inside out and print that skin.

Fingerprint detail is visible on the inner side of the skin as well as on the outside.

How the Victim Died

Once every effort has been made to get a positive identification of the fire victim, the next step is to determine how the victim died. First, X-rays are taken of the whole body. Looking at a badly burned body, the medical examiner cannot necessarily see bullet holes or stab wounds. "Someone could have been shot, stabbed, strangled or any number of things," explains McGee, "but if the skin is charred or badly burned, those wounds would not be obvious to us right away. These X-rays

Racism and Arson

One of the largest residential arson fires in recent history was racially motivated. In September 2005 a jury found twenty-one-year-old Patrick Walsh guilty of setting fire to a new housing development in a predominantly black community in southern Maryland in 2004. Walsh, who was part of an all-white gang who called themselves the Unseen Cavaliers, was believed to be the mastermind of the crime, which destroyed or damaged forty-one expensive houses under construction in a Charles County subdivision and caused an estimated $10 million in damage. One witness reported that Walsh had expressed outrage that black families were moving into the area and claimed burning the houses would drive them out.

will help determine whether any foreign metal objects—bullets, knife blades, and so on—are inside the body."[52]

While a stab wound or the presence of a bullet at an arson scene seem like obvious clues of a homicide, experts caution that they are not necessarily signs of crime. In one arson case, the body of a young woman with a deep chest wound was found in a burned trailer. Investigators learning that she and her husband had fought often, surmised that the husband had shot her and set the trailer on fire to hide the crime.

What the investigators discovered, however, pointed to a very different scenario. "We found that what had happened was purely accidental," says one forensic specialist:

Something was on the stove, she forgot about it, and went to sleep. She woke up, couldn't get out of the trailer because the exit from the bedroom was through the kitchen. She tried to use a scissors to get out the window—she was trying to cut the screen, and a dresser fell on her and she stabbed herself with the scissors. She didn't die from that wound, but because she couldn't get out of the trailer, she was overcome by smoke.[53]

Looking for Carbon Monoxide

After the X-rays, an autopsy is done to evaluate the condition of the internal organs. The medical examiner especially notes injuries or wounds to the heart, lungs, and other internal organs. If the internal organs are normal, it is likely that the person died because of smoke inhalation.

Asphyxia, the clinical term for suffocation due to inhaling smoke and carbon monoxide, (a dangerous gas produced

Medical examiners prepare to perform an autopsy in their lab to determine an arson victim's cause of death.

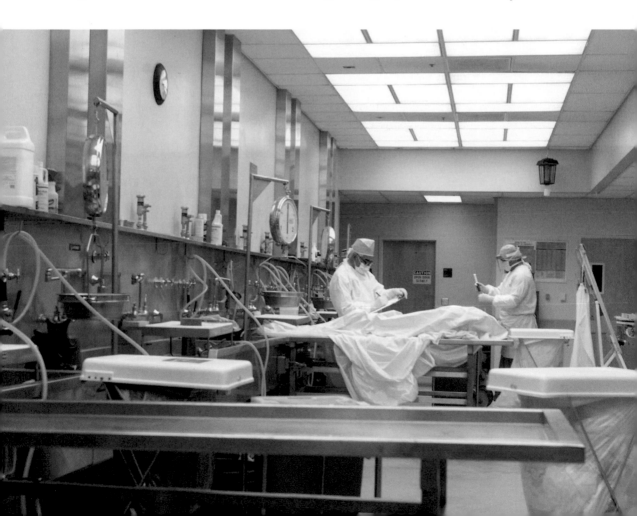

by fire) is by far the most common reason for fire deaths. Even a relatively small amount of carbon monoxide will force oxygen from the red blood cells and make it difficult for the body to get the oxygen it needs. Breathing air that contains only 1.3 percent carbon monoxide, for instance, will cause a person to lose consciousness in two breaths and die in a matter of minutes.

Forensic pathologists are interested in the level of carbon monoxide in the lungs and blood of a fire victim. A high level of carbon monoxide indicates that the victim was alive and breathing when the fire started. A low level suggests that the victim was already dead at the time of the fire. Homicide is

Fire victims are removed from the scene in body bags and taken to a medical examiner's office to be autopsied.

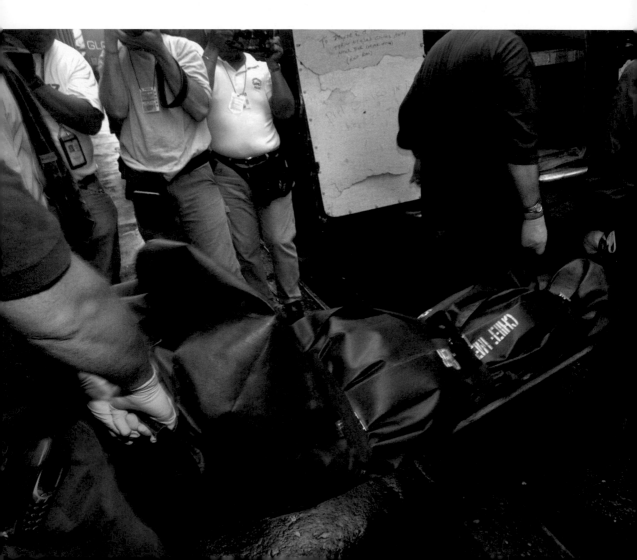

strongly considered if the victim was already dead when the fire started, for the murderer might have tried to cover the crime by setting a fire.

A toxicology screen, a lab test of blood and tissue samples from the body, will measure the level of carbon monoxide—in addition to showing the presence of any drugs, alcohol, or poisons. The toxicology screen uses the gas chromatograph and mass spectrometer, the same instruments that are used to detect accelerants in fire debris.

It is also common during an autopsy for medical examiners to be able to detect high carbon monoxide levels visually. "As you inhale [carbon monoxide], it combines with the hemoglobin in your red blood cells to produce *carboxyhemoglobin*, which is a bright red compound," explains forensic expert D.P. Lyle. "If the victim's blood, muscles, and organs are a bright, cherry-red color, the victim likely died from smoke and [carbon monoxide] inhalation."[54]

Where Was the Body Found?

The presence of high levels of carbon monoxide indicates that the victim was alive during the fire and that it was the fire that caused the death. The presence of soot in the nose, throat, and lungs is another sign that the victim was breathing during the fire. "It doesn't necessarily mean that the person was conscious, however," warns McGee. "The person may have been injured or wounded. They might have been breathing just enough to get that soot inside the airway. But if the person had been dead before the fire started, there would be no trace of it."[55]

The body's position is another way investigators determine the cause and manner of death. Most people who die in fires are found face down on the floor. That indicates that they might have been trying to get out of the building—either standing or crawling—and were overcome by smoke.

The unusual position of an elderly woman's body after a house fire in Edgewater, Florida, made investigators suspicious right away. Firefighters found the body sprawled face up on the bedroom floor. A subsequent autopsy failed to find any soot in the woman's nose or throat, indicating that she was dead before the fire began. The medical examiner was able to see bruising on her neck, which showed she had been strangled. This information alerted investigators that they needed to treat the fire as both an arson and a homicide.

The Value of DNA Evidence

Once homicide is suspected in a fatal fire, forensic pathologists take a careful look at the body, examining it as well as the clothing for trace evidence that might have survived the heat of the fire. At this time, the focus shifts from identifying the body and cause of death to looking for evidence that points to a particular suspect.

This model of a DNA strand shows the molecule's characteristic shape.

One of the most valuable tools in this search is DNA. DNA is found in the nucleus of the body's cells, and its long, double-helix-shaped strands contain information that is unique to each person. When scientists learned how to separate the DNA from the matter in which it was found (blood, hair, skin, semen, and so on), they began making DNA "fingerprints," or profiles. By matching the DNA fingerprint found in blood left at a crime scene to a suspect's DNA, for example, investigators could have positive proof that the suspect was at that scene.

Dr. McGee says that DNA has played a huge role in solving all sorts of crimes, and that is the one aspect of his job that has changed dramatically in the past ten years. "The way we do autopsies really hasn't changed a lot since the way they were done in the eighteenth century," he says. "What has changed is the capability of the forensic lab—especially when it comes to DNA. When I started, not so many years ago, if blood was found at a fire scene, for example, they could tell us what type it was—A, B, like that. And that's about all they could do.

"DNA was done back then," McGee adds, "but it was expensive and therefore done in only the most special cases. Also, it was inconvenient

Becoming a DNA Specialist

Job Description:

A DNA specialist is responsible for conducting DNA analysis, communicating with police or other law enforcement officers, identifying and comparing biological samples, writing case reports, and testifying in court as an expert witness.

Education:

An applicant must have a college degree in biology, chemistry, biochemistry, molecular biology, genetics, or a related field. Employers usually prefer that a DNA specialist also have earned a master's degree in one of these fields.

DNA specialists analyze DNA found at crime scenes in order to identify both victims and suspects.

Qualifications:

An applicant must have thorough knowledge of various laws pertaining to the gathering and testing of evidence, along with effective oral and written communication skills. A DNA specialist also must be able to manage and supervise laboratory staff and demonstrate excellent computer skills.

Salary:

With a bachelor of science degree, between $40,000 and $80,000 per year. With a master's degree, between $48,000 and $90,000 per year.

and slow, because all the cases had to be done in Washington, D.C. It took forever to get results back. Now we have DNA labs locally that can do the work quickly."[56]

"It's a Habit"

Crime scene crews at fires have begun to look for DNA as a matter of course, just as they do at homicide scenes. "You see a pop can or a beer bottle, you think fingerprint, and at the same time, you think DNA," says forensic expert Steve Banning. "It's a habit with me. If a suspect drank out of that can or bottle, chances are there's going to be a trace of saliva on the very inside of it, so I swab it.

"Or if I see a match book, or even a match, there might be skin cells that have sloughed off. You can't really tell by looking—this is stuff you'd need a microscope to see. Just like on a door handle of a car door or a house. Little microscopic bits of skin are shed all the time."[57]

Crews at the scene of a suspicious fire carry a kit especially for gathering DNA evidence. The kit contains a collection of vials of different sizes as well as precision tweezers that are capable of picking up a single strand of hair. The kit also contains gloves, a magnifying glass, and a container of sterile water. "You use the water to swab something dry, like a car door handle," Banning explains. "You don't need to wet the swab if you're getting a sample of something that's already wet, like blood. Then you put the sample in a vial, label it, and take it back to the lab. For all you know, the blood or hair could belong to the victim, but you never know."[58]

Autorads and "Growing DNA"

In the crime lab, the samples of blood, saliva, or other DNA-loaded material are treated with chemicals to separate them from the DNA. The DNA is coiled very tightly in the nucleus of each cell, but if it were unrolled it would be about 6 feet (1.8m) long. Not all of the DNA is important in the crime lab, however.

Most of the hereditary information in DNA is detail that is common to all humans, but there are small sections that contain information that is unique to an individual. Those sections are printed on a sheet of special photographic film. When developed, the image—called an autorad—looks very much like a blurry bar code on a grocery store item. A person's autorad can be scanned by a computer and then compared to a DNA sample provided by a suspect—or put through DNA databases to see if it matches a sample already on file.

One of the early drawbacks of using DNA in the lab was that often the trace evidence did not provide an adequate sample to test. Perhaps it was too small, or it was damaged from the heat of the fire. However, scientists have discovered a method of "growing" a complete DNA chain in the laboratory from a partial sample. Known as PCR (short for polymerase chain reaction), this method mimics the cell's ability to replicate its own DNA material.

Swimming Pool–Sized DNA

"Once we know the pattern from the sample we have," says Banning, "we now have the technology to replicate the pattern until we have enough to analyze. From a single piece of DNA, we could duplicate that material more and more—to the size of a swimming pool, if need be."[59]

Medical examiners and forensic scientists hail this technique as one of the most important new tools in the crime lab. "With PCR amplification, the advancement of DNA is enormous," says McGee. "Information that previously was not of any value is of tremendous value now. What we're looking for, like single hairs,

Magnifying glasses (far left) and tweezers are used to obtain very small clues from crime scenes.

Forensic experts create film records of DNA that can be examined during arson investigations.

small drops of blood, cigarette butts, traces of saliva from a telephone receiver—any of that material may contain DNA."[60]

And while processing and analyzing DNA is much quicker than in years past, forensic experts predict that very soon crime scene technicians will have a handheld DNA instrument that will allow them to identify the source of a drop of blood, a hair, or some other material containing DNA on the spot, rather than having to take evidence back to a laboratory to be run on a computer. Says Banning, "When that happens, it will be a tremendous edge for law enforcement."[61]

CHAPTER 5

Going Beyond Science

There is no question that forensic science is an invaluable tool in solving arson cases. However, forensic science is only one of the tools that investigators use to solve arson cases. Another important way of investigating is by profiling a fire. That means that police try to understand what might have motivated a person to purposely set the fire. In many cases, finding out the motive behind the fire can lead investigators to a suspect.

Revenge Fires

A very common motive for arson is revenge. "Person A is mad because Person B owes them money," says Dale, a police officer. "A lot of the time that's what sets it off. An unpaid debt, a conflict over territory between rival gangs, whatever. Burning down someone's apartment or house gets their attention. [The arsonist does not] need to get a gun and shoot anybody, but it's a strong message."[62]

One such fire, with tragic results, occurred in St. Paul, Minnesota, on a wintry February night in 1994. Members of a gang known as the 6-0-Tre Crips threw a firebomb into the home of a fellow gang member, fifteen-year-old Andre Coppage. The arsonists mistakenly believed that Coppage had broken the gang's code of silence by talking to police about a recent killing. Coppage survived the blaze, but his five brothers and sisters, ages two to eleven, died in the fire.

"There's a lot of us who still have nightmares about that one," says one St. Paul firefighter. "Some of those kids that died were really little—still in their cribs. It was a horrible, horrible scene. When that happened, ten years ago, my two kids were the same ages as the youngest ones. [The victims] never had a chance—call it a revenge fire, but who paid the price?"[63]

In order to solve an arson crime, investigators consider not just the forensic evidence but the possible motives for setting the fire.

Sometimes the motive is revenge directed not against a person, but against an institution. Someone who has been evicted from an apartment or fired from a job might be angry enough to set a fire to get even. One graduate assistant in a university chemistry department was furious that she had been passed over for a promotion. Investigators believe that to strike out at university officials who she thought had treated her unfairly, she intentionally set fire to a chemistry lab, causing more than a million dollars' worth of damage.

Bowling Trophies

Relationship breakups are another frequent cause of arson fires. "Sometimes a guy will be so angry at his wife or girlfriend that he takes her clothes out of the closet and just heaps them up on the bed," says one crime scene technician. "He puts gas or lighter fluid or something on the pile of clothes and lets them burn. A lot of the time, we'll get there and find a lot of charred clothing, and metal hangers that didn't burn."[64]

Arsonists sometimes target private residences as acts of revenge.

Investigators say that these crimes are often the easiest to solve—not necessarily because of something they find at the crime scene, but because of what they do not find. Many such arsonists will take great pains to remove their own clothing

or possessions from the scene before starting the fire. Even a novice investigator can see that something is odd about a fire that destroys the possessions of only one member of the household. One lab technician says that she once viewed a fire scene where a woman had piled her husband's sports equipment in the basement and lit it: "She had even dumped golf clubs and a couple of bowling trophies in there from ten years ago."[65]

Fire for Profit

Another common motive for arson is money. Some people intentionally set fire to their belongings to collect insurance money. Automobiles are the most common target of arson in cases like this. In 2002, more than sixty thousand cases of automobile arson occurred in the United States.

"Cars are a real big target for insurance fraud fires," agrees arson investigator Sean McKenna. "Someone has a nice car, truck, whatever—and all of a sudden there's problems with the engine or something. But it's going to cost more to fix the thing than it's worth. So they set it on fire, and hope to collect a nice bit of insurance. What happens is that they call in that their car's been stolen, and we find the thing in some big park at four in the morning, burning away."[66]

The Human Toll of Arson

Because of the high financial costs of arson, people sometimes forget that the crime has a human cost, too. Each year, hundreds of deaths and thousands of injuries—many life-changing—result from arson fires. Myiesha Hicks is an example. On June 2, 2000, drug dealers drove by her family's Detroit home and threw a firebomb into her bedroom. Four-year-old Myiesha suffered third-degree burns on her face, hands, and arms. Her organs swelled, she had trouble breathing, and the severe damage to her skin made her very vulnerable to infection.

Doctors set out to repair her skin by performing a series of skin grafts, transplanting skin from her back to her face, scalp, arms, and hands. A year after the crime, Myiesha's face was marked by stitches and scars from multiple grafts. Her parents say her scars are not only physical: She is emotionally and socially scarred as well, terribly shy and self-conscious among other children, and angry about what happened to her. This too, say experts, is the face of arson.

Arsonists will set fire to vehicles in order to collect insurance money.

Homes and businesses are also targets of arsonists who are having financial difficulties. "One man's business was losing almost $1,000 a week," says forensic expert Dave Tebow, "and that insurance payoff from a fire would solve his problem. That's one of the key things a good investigator looks at—does anyone benefit from the fire? If the answer is that the owner would benefit most, that points to someone as a suspect."[67]

Arson for Gratification

A great many fires are set by people who find it a thrilling experience. For young arsonists especially, the idea of creating something as large and destructive as a fire gives them a feeling of power they lack in their everyday lives. "Not only is the fire itself exciting to these individuals," says one firefighter, "but the whole thing that happens when the fire is reported. You get fire engines, sirens, flashing lights, the whole works. And crowds of people watching—and it's all because of something they did. For them it's a rush."[68]

California serial arsonist John Orr reportedly found a different sort of gratification in the fires he set. As an arson investigator, he was frequently called out to examine suspicious fire scenes, and because he had set many of the fires himself, he used those opportunities to become a hero. Fellow investigators say he could put his finger on a time-delay ignition device when others had scoured the area in vain, or he could walk right to the point of origin—even at the scene of a wildfire.

Rich Edwards of the Los Angeles County Sheriffs Department said that when investigators finally learned about Orr's arson activities, there was a part of him that was not surprised:

> Over time, John would arrive and quickly go to the area of origin. I found it a coincidence that in many of these fires, John quickly recovered an incendiary device that he believed had started the fire. As an experienced investigator, I know how hard it was to do that and was

initially impressed. As time went on that little voice spoke inside me, which comes with experience . . . and the hair stood up on the back of my neck, and I just started to wonder.[69]

Relaxed Interviews

As in the John Orr case, the motive is not always known when an arson investigation begins. That is why investigators try to develop a list of suspects who might have had some reason to set the fire and to meet with each of them individually. McKenna feels that interviewing suspects is an important tool in the investigation. By asking the right questions during the interview, a good investigator can get a sense of whether the suspect is telling the truth.

"I like to interview someone in a public place, odd as that may sound," he says. "I think people are a little more open in public, sitting around having a cup of coffee. They're more relaxed. The TV stuff, where detectives are pounding on tables,

Investigators interview witnesses and victims extensively in an attempt to discover an arsonist.

yelling—that doesn't really work in an arson investigation.

"You really get better results if you befriend people. It's not often you get a confession, either," McKenna warns. "Arson is one of the crimes that gets the least number of convictions because it is so difficult to prove. Lots of times, you are successful if you can get them to settle [pay back the damage they did] when they're guilty. Except in cases where someone dies—and the homicide people get involved, too—we in the arson unit have to be content with that."[70]

Investigators acknowledge that the ways they unravel the stories of suspects differ from case to case. They say that there might sometimes be one little thread, one little piece of a story that can be disproved or questioned. "It's just a matter of a suspect talking, talking, telling you something you know is wrong, and the lies just build up," says McKenna. "Guilty people tend to get tangled up in their own lies—they can't keep their story straight. Finally they end up saying something that we can verify is false. And the prosecuting attorney says, 'Yep, you've got it.' Then we know we have a shot."[71]

The detailed interviews conducted by insurance agents can help lead investigators to an arsonist.

Help from Many Places

Several sources of information can help investigators build a case against a suspect. In fires for profit, insurance agents are often helpful partners. Insurance companies require that the insured person participate in interviews until the company is satisfied that the fire was not intentionally set. While arsonists are usually unwilling to continue speaking with police investigators unless they are under arrest, they have to satisfy the questions of insurance investigators if they want to have their claims paid.

It is a powerful bargaining tool for the insurance company, for the person making a claim must give a deposition under oath. The person must tell the truth, for any statement that is found to be false can result in the company's refusal to pay anything. In one 2002 case a Minnesota man who police were certain had burned his own truck to collect the insurance was asked by the police at the deposition whether he had ever been convicted of a felony. The man said no.

"Well, we had reason to believe that he *had* been convicted of burglary in California," says McKenna. "The guy said no, that that was his brother. So I called the Long Beach Department of Corrections and had them send me a photo of the guy who'd done time for burglary. They sent it back right away, and it was my guy. I gave it to the insurance investigator, since my case [the police investigation] wasn't going anywhere. They realized he had lied, and they refused to pay for a $20,000 Chevy Suburban. And the guy was left with nothing."[72]

Witnesses can provide information to investigators that seems unimportant but is actually crucial evidence.

The Power of Witnesses

Another type of help that investigators value is the statements of witnesses. In fact, in most cases where arsonists are tried and convicted, a witness has provided key testimony. For example, when a Michigan couple's home burned down in 1999, they submitted an insurance claim, listing all of their expensive possessions as having been destroyed in the blaze. But a sharp-eyed neighbor alerted investigators that the couple had loaded their van with clothes, photograph albums, stereo equipment, and other valuables before the fire started.

Sometimes the witnesses are former friends or associates of the arsonist who decide later to come forward, as in the case of a rural Florida fire in 2002. Investigators had ruled the fire that destroyed a house accidental, but a year afterward, a young woman came to police with a different story.

> **By the Numbers**
>
> # 55
> **Percentage of arson fires set by persons under 21 years of age**

She said that her boyfriend had set the fire to destroy a rival drug dealer's home. She also gave investigators a key piece of information that led them to a gasoline-stained coat in the back of a closet. The woman had known that her boyfriend was planning to set the fire, but she did nothing to stop him at the time. However, when they broke up, she realized she had no reason to be loyal to him any longer and told police the story.

Following the Paper Trail

In addition to talking with witnesses, arson investigators can learn a great deal by examining what is called the paper trail—receipts, bills, bank statements, insurance papers, and other documents that may help unravel lies in a suspect's story. In fact, say investigators, the piece of evidence that turns an arson case may be a bill or other document.

"Again, it's that thing about catching the suspect in a lie," says McKenna. "If someone who is considered a suspect claims they were in Chicago or something the night the fire started, and you find receipts or other documents that can place them here, not Chicago, then you've started unraveling their story."[73]

In the case of a young Minnesota man accused of setting his apartment building on fire in 2001, cell phone records made the difference to investigators. The man was already considered a suspect in the fire for a couple of reasons: he had had arguments with the landlord, who had threatened to evict him, and he had once set a vehicle on fire for insurance purposes.

"The individual claimed he was out of town that night— said he was at his mother's home in Florida," says one police officer who worked on the case:

> He insisted that we were picking on him for his previous mistake, and said that his mother would verify that he was with her that night.
>
> But when we got the cell phone company to turn over his records for that time period, it was clear he was in town after all. We made a list of all the calls from that day, and we saw that he had made lots of them. We knew he made a call to order a pizza from a local place and had talked to numerous friends on that phone. Then we cross-checked, talking to the pizza guy and some of the friends, and we had confirmation that he was in town. There was no way that he was in Florida that night.[74]

"The Fires You Never Forget"

While phone records or other data can sometimes give investigators the clue that points to a suspect's involvement in an arson fire, many investigations seem to go nowhere, despite

The Firefighting Arsonist

All arson is dismaying, but arson fires set by firefighters strike investigators and the public alike as particularly outrageous. In February 2005, for instance, Chicago fire lieutenant Jeffrey Boyle was charged with setting at least eight fires in the city and surrounding area. Most of the blazes were set in garages, construction sites, and trash bins. Boyle told detectives that he has suffered from depression for several years, and that the condition resulted in an overwhelming compulsion to set fires. He cited various events as triggers—breaking up with his girlfriend, legal troubles, and losing money in a Super Bowl wager.

In an article in the *Chicago Tribune,* reporters David Heinzmann and Jeff Coen quote an arson investigator who said that Boyle admitted that he "did stupid things at different times. . . . He would drive around and wouldn't feel right, and would want to start a fire."

the best efforts of police and lab technicians. "Things just seem to stall—a lack of a witness or a suspect that you can't find any threads to unravel in their story," says McKenna. "When that happens and other cases happen, you don't forget it, you put it on the back burner and hope something shakes out later. And we've had cases where that has happened—it's stalled one minute and the next you are in business."

As an example, McKenna cites a series of fires that occurred in the mid-1990s in a residential area of Minneapolis. "There were between forty and eighty fires in a two-block by two-block area. For most of them, it was always the same MC [routine used in committing a crime]—someone would take a mattress from the yard and lean it up against a building and set it on fire. Those things smolder for a while, then they touch off after an hour or so.

"You have to understand," he says:

this is a part of town where when people move, they can't afford a moving van. With big stuff, like mattresses, they tend to leave them. The new tenants tend to toss them out in the yard, and let the landlord deal with it.

Anyway, the fires were always early in the morning, and no one ever saw anything. One fire in particular was really bad—a mattress was left against a big sixplex apartment building. A little girl was crippled from it— she suffered a brain injury because she'd gone without oxygen for too long. She spent six months in the hospital—it was that bad. Another girl who had been sleeping over at her house was badly burned. And still we had nothing—and it was very, very frustrating. Those are the fires you never forget, when people— especially kids—are hurt or killed. But we had nothing.

It was years later, McKenna says, that he got a break in the case. A police officer from a nearby suburb said that he had a suspect in custody for starting a fire, and the man wanted to talk about other fires he had set.

"The thing is, he wanted to help himself, maybe get a lesser sentence by confessing to prior crimes," McKenna says. "He ended up explaining that he and his brother had set that fire, the one with the girls. I know these guys probably did all the fires, but that was the one we were talking about. He insisted that it was his brother who set the fire, even though he was there, too. His brother was convicted of that one and sentenced to ten years in prison."[75] The brother who confessed received a far lighter sentence.

"It's a Partnership"

Arson experts say that the low conviction rate for arson is disheartening. Arson fires usually occur at night, out of sight of

Conviction rates for arson are low because eyewitness testimony is often lacking and because fires often damage physical evidence.

witnesses. And fires are, obviously, damaging to potential forensic evidence. These characteristics of fires often make arson investigation a discouraging job.

But while the statistics of cases solved and arsonists convicted are not as high as those for other felonies, arson experts are confident that those numbers will improve. For example, many arson investigators are excited about education programs that teach communities about the heavy financial and human costs of arson fires. Some police departments hold regular meetings in parks and community centers, explaining to people how the neighborhoods themselves can help solve arson cases.

"A big part of my work has become communication with neighborhoods," says McKenna. "I put up fliers and signs in neighborhoods where there's been a recent suspicious fire. We want people to call, we want them to get involved by telling us when they see something suspicious."[76]

In addition, new technology in the crime lab is making technicians' jobs easier. "On the forensic side," says chemist Steve Banning, "we've seen advances in the last ten years that continue to make our work more accurate, where we can do more in evaluating evidence with less of a sample." The lab technicians can thus provide a full report to police investigators more quickly than before. "That's the best way to deal with a violent crime like arson," says Banning. "I said it before, I'll say it again. It's a partnership between science and police investigators, and I'm really optimistic that we all can substantially reduce the numbers of arson fires."[77]

Notes

Introduction: "I Can't Think of Anything More Terrible"

1. Personal interview, Cora Seels, September 1, 2004, Minneapolis, MN.

2. Personal interview, Dan (last name withheld), October 15, 2004, Young America, MN.

3. Quoted in Nicholas Faith, *Blaze: The Forensics of Fire.* New York: St. Martin's, 1999, p. 85.

4. Quoted in Faith, *Blaze,* p. 9.

Chapter 1: Establishing a Crime

5. Telephone interview, Tom Hall, November 16, 2004.

6. Dan, October 15, 2004.

7. Quoted in Faith, *Blaze,* p. 63.

8. Dan, October 15, 2004.

9. Personal interview, Sean McKenna, September 30, 2004, Minneapolis, MN.

10. McKenna, September 30, 2004.

11. McKenna, September 30, 2004.

12. McKenna, September 30, 2004.

13. Telephone interview, Sean McKenna, October 11, 2004.

14. Hall, November 16, 2004.

15. Quoted in Faith, *Blaze,* p. 11.

16. Telephone interview, Bill (last name withheld), November 21, 2004.

17. McKenna, September 30, 2004.

Chapter 2: Gathering Forensic Evidence

18. Hall, November 16, 2004.

19. Personal inteview, Dave Tebow, November 4, 2004, St. Paul, MN.

20. Quoted in Kelly Andersson, "Arson Dogs," *Working Dogs Cyberzine,* 1997. www.workingdogs.com/doc0130htm.

21. Quoted in "Chemical Detectives," *Assignment: Discovery* (video). Bethesda, MD: Discovery Channel School, 2002.

22. Quoted in Andersson, "Arson Dogs."

23. Tebow, November 4, 2004.

24. McKenna, September 30, 2004.

25. Tebow, November 4, 2004.

26. Personal interview, Steve Banning, November 9, 2004, St. Paul, MN.

27. Banning, November 9, 2004.

28. Banning, November 9, 2004.

29. D.P. Lyle, *Forensics for Dummies,* Hoboken, NJ: Wiley 2004, p. 101.

30. Banning, November 9, 2004.

31. Tebow, November 4, 2004.

32. Bill, November 21, 2004.

33. Banning, November 9, 2004.

Chapter 3: Analyzing the Evidence

34. Telephone interview, Amy (last name withheld), November 10, 2004.

35. McKenna, September 30, 2004.

36. Personal interview, Dave Tebow, December 6, 2004.

37. Quoted in Faith, *Blaze,* p. 128.

38. Personal interview, Curt (last name withheld), November 29, 2004, Minneapolis, MN.

39. John Houde, *Crime Lab: A Guide for Nonscientists.* Ventura, CA: Calico, 1999, p. 79.

40. Tebow, November 4, 2004.

41. Tebow, November 4, 2004.

42. Tebow, November 4, 2004.

43. Personal interview, Dale (last name withheld), December 1, 2004, St. Paul, MN.

Chapter 4: Investigating Fatal Fires

44. Personal interview, Dr. Michael McGee, December 8, 2004, St. Paul, MN.

45. McGee, December 8, 2004.

46. McGee, December 8, 2004.

47. McGee, December 8, 2004.

48. Dale, December 1, 2004.

49. Bill, November 21, 2004.

50. Amy, November 10, 2004.

51. David Fisher, *Hard Evidence: How Detectives Inside the FBI's Sci-Crime Lab Have Helped Solve America's Toughest Cases.* New York: Simon and Schuster, 1995. p. 145.

52. McGee, December 8, 2004.

53. Banning, November 9, 2004.

54. Lyle, *Forensics for Dummies,* p. 124.

55. McGee, December 8, 2004.

56. McGee, December 8, 2004.

57. Banning, November 9, 2004.

58. Banning, November 9, 2004.

59. Banning, November 9, 2004.

60. McGee, December 8, 2004.

61. Banning, November 9, 2004.

Chapter 5: Going Beyond Science

62. Dale, December 1, 2004.

63. Personal interview, name withheld, November 18, 2004, St. Paul, MN.

64. Amy, November 10, 2004.

65. Amy, November 10, 2004.

66. McKenna, September 30, 2004.

67. Tebow, November 4, 2004.

68. Dan, October 15, 2004.

69. Quoted in Faith, *Blaze*, p. 129.

70. McKenna, September 30, 2004.

71. McKenna, September 30, 2004.

72. McKenna, September 30, 2004.

73. McKenna, September 30, 2004.

74. Personal interview, name withheld, December 10, 2004, St. Paul, MN.

75. McKenna, September 30, 2004.

76. McKenna, September 30, 2004.

77. Banning, November 9, 2004.

For Further Reading

Books

David Owen, *Hidden Evidence: Forty True Crimes and How Forensic Science Helped Solve Them*. Buffalo, NY: Firefly, 2000. Helpful information on the scanning electron microscope and how it is used in solving crimes.

Katherine Ramsland, *The Forensic Science of C.S.I.* New York: Berkley, 2001. Very helpful glossary.

Jenny Tesar, *Scientific Crime Investigation*. New York: Franklin Watts, 1991. Though some material is dated, the book contains a good section on fingerprint analysis.

Joseph Wambaugh, *Fire Lover*. New York: William Morrow, 2002. Fascinating account of the John Orr case in California.

Tabatha Yeatts, *Forensics: Solving the Crime*. Minneapolis: Oliver, 2001. Excellent chapter on the development of DNA analysis and the amplification of DNA samples.

Periodicals and Web Sites

Michelle Hunter, "Murder Precedes Fire in Jefferson Garage," *New Orleans Times-Picayune*, May 27, 2004. Interfire online. www.interfire.org.

Works Consulted

Books

Nicholas Faith, *Blaze: The Forensics of Fire*. New York: St. Martin's, 1999. Well-written, with good background on several devastating fires throughout the world and how they were investigated.

David Fisher, *Hard Evidence: How Detectives Inside the FBI's Sci-Crime Lab Have Helped Solve America's Toughest Cases*. New York: Simon & Schuster, 1995. Very interesting material on identifying arson fatalities.

John Houde, *Crime Lab: A Guide for Nonscientists*. Ventura, CA: Calico, 1999. Excellent photographs and very helpful sections on tool marks and the gas chromatograph.

D.P. Lyle, *Forensics for Dummies*. Hoboken, NJ: Wiley, 2004. Very readable chapters on DNA and autopsies.

David Owen, *Police Lab: How Forensic Science Tracks Down and Convicts Criminals*. Buffalo, NY: Firefly, 2002. Excellent illustrations and photographs, with a helpful index.

David R. Redsicker and John J. O'Connor, *Practical Fire and Arson Investigation*, 2nd ed. New York: CRC, 1997. Good material, although photographs of fire fatalities are very graphic and may upset readers.

Periodicals, Videos, and Web Sites

Kelly Andersson, "Arson Dogs," *Working Dogs Cyberzine*, 1997. www.working dogs.com/doc0130.htm.

"Chemical Detectives," *Assignment: Discovery* (video). Bethesda, MD: Discovery Channel School, 2002.

David Heinzmann and Jeff Coen, "Fire Official Set Blazes When Upset, Cops Say," *Chicago Tribune*, February 11, 2005.

Ellise Pierce, "The Hot Light of Heroism," *Newsweek*, May 12, 2003.

Index

accelerants, 23, 30–32

accidental fires, 21–23, 24–25

alligator skin, 20

arson

  case characteristics in, 13

  conviction rate for, 90–92

  description of, by victim, 6–7

  dollar cost of loss due to, 8, 23

  evidence destruction in, 10–11

  gangs and, 78

  motives for, 78–84

  racism and, 68

  statistics for, 8

  as violent crime, 8–9

  see also arsonists; arson statistics

arson dogs, 31–32, 51

arsonists

  age statistics for, 87

  behavioral clues and, 17–18

  conviction rates for, 10

  fire delaying devices used by, 34–35

  firefighters as, 50–51, 89

  as heroes, 83–84

  motives of, 78–80

  psychology of, 12, 18

  racism and, 68

  as spectators, 16

  tools of, 23–24, 58–59

  volunteer firefighters as, 18

  as witnesses, 16, 17

  see also motivations

asphyxia, 69–70

ATF. See Bureau of Alcohol, Tobacco, and Firearms

Automatic Fingerprint Identification System (AFIS), 47, 49, 66

automobile fires, 81

autopsies

  challenges of, 62

  dental identification and, 63–65

  purpose of, 60

  urgency in, 62

autorad. *See* DNA evidence

Avato, Steve, 9

Banning, Steve

  on collaborative nature of investigation, 92

  on DNA collection, 74, 77

  on forensic technology advances, 92

  on searching for evidence, 35–36, 43

bifurcations, 49

blood type, 72

Boyle, Jeffrey, 89

Bureau of Alcohol, Tobacco, and Firearms (ATF), 9, 31

Bureau of Criminal Apprehension (BCA), 32

burn pattern, 20

burns, 81

Picture Credits

Cover image (main): AP Images

AP Images, 7, 12, 25, 26, 29, 51, 61, 80, 84, 91 (inset and main)

Billy Hustace/Getty Images, 33

David McCarthy/Photo Researchers, Inc., 65

© Earl Cryer/ZUMA/CORBIS, 41 (background)

© EggImages/Alamy, 16

© Frances M. Roberts/Alamy, 70

Getty Images, 11, 67, 82

Joseph Paris, 18, 39, 54–55 (left to right)

Julie Plasencia/San Francisco Chronicle/CORBIS, 69

© Mark Peterson/CORBIS, 45

© Matthias Kulka/zefa/CORBIS, 72

Mauro Fermariello/Photo Researchers, Inc., 53, 56, 76

Maury Aaseng, 9, 19, 41, 63

Michael Donne/Photo Researchers, Inc., 14, 34

© Michael Goulding/Orange County Register/CORBIS, 10

© Michael Maass, 48, 57, 73

© Mikael Karlsson/Alamy, 46–47 (left to right), 86

© Mikael Karlsson/Arresting Images, 64

© Mike/zefa/CORBIS, 42

PhotoDisc, 74

Photos.com, 15, 58, 63 (background), 75

© Shout/Alamy, 22, 24, 35

TEK Image/Photo Researchers, Inc., 52

The Image Bank/Getty Images, 79, 85

About the Author

Gail B. Stewart received her undergraduate degree from Gustavus Adolphus College in St. Peter, Minnesota. She did her graduate work in English, linguistics, and curriculum study at the College of St. Thomas and the University of Minnesota. She taught English and reading for more than ten years.

She has written over ninety books for young people, including a series for Lucent Books called The Other America. She has written many books on historical topics such as World War I and the Warsaw ghetto.

Stewart and her husband live in Minneapolis with their three sons, Ted, Elliot, and Flynn; two dogs; and a cat. When Stewart is not writing, she enjoys reading, walking, and watching her sons play soccer.